iPod® & iTunes®

VISUAL™
Quick Tips

Visual®

by Kate Shoup

BICENTENNIAL
1807
WILEY
2007
BICENTENNIAL

Wiley Publishing, Inc.

iPod® & iTunes® VISUAL™ Quick Tips

Published by

Wiley Publishing, Inc.

111 River Street

Hoboken, NJ 07030-5774

Published simultaneously in Canada

Copyright © 2007 by Wiley Publishing, Inc., Indianapolis, Indiana

Library of Congress Control Number: 2007935021

978-0-470-18012-9

Manufactured in the United States of America

10 9 8 7 6 5 4 3 2 1

Trademark Acknowledgments

Contact Us

For general information on our other products and services contact our Customer Care Department within the U.S. at 800-762-2974, outside the U.S. at 317-572-3993, or fax 317-572-4002.

For technical support please visit www.wiley.com/techsupport.

WILEY

Wiley Publishing, Inc.

Sales

Contact Wiley at (800) 762-2974 or fax (317) 572-4002.

Praise for Visual Books

"I have to praise you and your company on the fine products you turn out. I have twelve Visual books in my house. They were instrumental in helping me pass a difficult computer course. Thank you for creating books that are easy to follow. Keep turning out those quality books."
Gordon Justin (Brielle, NJ)

"What fantastic teaching books you have produced! Congratulations to you and your staff. You deserve the Nobel prize in Education. Thanks for helping me understand computers."
Bruno Tonon (Melbourne, Australia)

"A Picture Is Worth A Thousand Words! If your learning method is by observing or hands-on training, this is the book for you!"
Lorri Pegan-Durastante (Wickliffe, OH)

"Over time, I have bought a number of your 'Read Less - Learn More' books. For me, they are THE way to learn anything easily. I learn easiest using your method of teaching."
José A. Mazón (Cuba, NY)

"You've got a fan for life!! Thanks so much!!"
Kevin P. Quinn (Oakland, CA)

"I have several books from the Visual series and have always found them to be valuable resources."
Stephen P. Miller (Ballston Spa, NY)

"I have several of your Visual books and they are the best I have ever used."
Stanley Clark (Crawfordville, FL)

"Like a lot of other people, I understand things best when I see them visually. Your books really make learning easy and life more fun."
John T. Frey (Cadillac, MI)

"I have quite a few of your Visual books and have been very pleased with all of them. I love the way the lessons are presented!"
Mary Jane Newman (Yorba Linda, CA)

"Thank you, thank you, thank you...for making it so easy for me to break into this high-tech world."
Gay O'Donnell (Calgary, Alberta,Canada)

"I write to extend my thanks and appreciation for your books. They are clear, easy to follow, and straight to the point. Keep up the good work! I bought several of your books and they are just right! No regrets! I will always buy your books because they are the best."
Seward Kollie (Dakar, Senegal)

"I would like to take this time to thank you and your company for producing great and easy-to-learn products. I bought two of your books from a local bookstore, and it was the best investment I've ever made! Thank you for thinking of us ordinary people."
Jeff Eastman (West Des Moines, IA)

"Compliments to the chef!! Your books are extraordinary! Or, simply put, extra-ordinary, meaning way above the rest! THANKYOU THANKYOU THANKYOU! I buy them for friends, family, and colleagues."
Christine J. Manfrin (Castle Rock, CO)

Credits

Project Editor
Chris Wolfgang

Acquisitions Editor
Jody Lefevere

Copy Editor
Marylouise Wiack

Technical Editor
Dennis Cohen

Editorial Manager
Robyn Siesky

Business Manager
Amy Knies

Sr. Marketing Manger
Sandy Smith

Manufacturing
Allan Conley
Linda Cook
Paul Gilchrist
Jennifer Guynn

Book Design
Kathie Rickard

Cover Design
Anthony Bunyan

Production Coordinator
Adrienne Martinez

Layout
Carrie A. Cesavice
Jennifer Mayberry
Amanda Spagnuolo

Screen Artist
Jill A. Proll

Illustrators
Ronda David-Burroughs
Cheryl Grubbs

Proofreader
Broccoli Information Management

Quality Control
Cynthia Fields

Indexer
Broccoli Information Management

Vice President and Executive Group Publisher
Richard Swadley

Vice President and Publisher
Barry Pruett

Composition Director
Debbie Stailey

Wiley Bicentennial Logo
Richard J. Pacifico

ABOUT THE AUTHOR

During the course of her career as a freelance writer, **Kate Shoup** has written or co-written several books on various topics, including *Look & Learn FrontPage 2002*, *What Can You Do with a Major in Business*, *Not Your Mama's Beading*, *Not Your Mama's Stitching*, *Windows Vista Visual Encyclopedia*, *Teach Yourself Visually Outlook 2007*, and *Webster's New World English Grammar Handbook*. She has also co-written a screenplay, and worked as the Sports Editor for *NUVO Newsweekly*. Prior to striking out on her own, Kate worked as an editor at a computer-publishing company, where she engaged in such diverse professional activities as consulting on the development of new series, consulting on ways to improve the publishing workflow, and editing numerous standout titles. When not writing, Kate loves to ski (she was once nationally ranked), make jewelry, and play video poker — and she plays a mean game of 9-ball. Kate lives in Indianapolis with her daughter.

AUTHOR ACKNOWLEDGMENTS

The publication of any book is an enormous undertaking, involving many people, and this one is no exception. Thanks are due to Jody Lefevere for providing me with the opportunity to write this book, to Chris Wolfgang for her expert guidance during the writing process, to Dennis Cohen for his technical expertise, and to Marylouise Wiack for catching my numerous grammatical slip-ups. Thanks, too, to the book's production team. Finally, thanks to my family (especially my daughter Heidi) and friends — you know who you are.

How To Use This Book

iPod & iTunes VISUAL Quick Tips includes 104 tasks that reveal cool secrets, teach timesaving tricks, and explain great tips guaranteed to make you more productive with your iPod as well as iTunes. The easy-to-use layout lets you work through all the tasks from beginning to end or jump in at random.

Who is this book for?

If you want to know the basics about using a video iPod, or if you want to learn shortcuts, tricks, and tips that let you maneuver seamlessly through iTunes, this book is for you. And because it can be easier to learn when someone *shows* you how, this is the book for you.

Conventions Used In This Book

❶ Introduction
The introduction is designed to get you up to speed on the topic at hand.

❷ Steps
This book uses step-by-step instructions to guide you easily through each task. Numbered callouts on every screen shot show you exactly how to perform each task, step by step.

❸ Tips
Practical tips provide insights to save you time and trouble, caution you about hazards to avoid, and reveal how to do things on your iPod and with iTunes that you never thought possible!

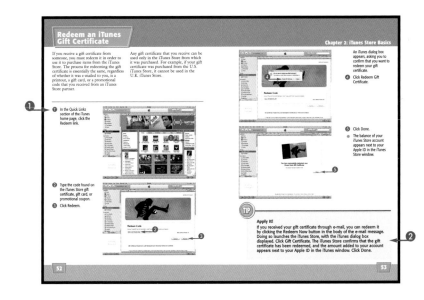

Table of Contents

chapter 1 iTunes Basics

chapter 2 iTunes Store Basics

chapter 3

iPod Basics

chapter 4 Enjoy Music with iTunes and Your iPod

chapter 5 Work with Playlists and Burn CDs with iTunes

chapter 6 **Enjoy Other Audio Content with iTunes and Your iPod**

chapter 7 **Enjoy Video with iTunes and Your iPod**

chapter 8

Explore iPod Extras

chapter **9** Manage Your iTunes Library

iTunes Basics

iTunes, a digital media player introduced by Apple in 2001, is designed to enable users to perform many media-oriented tasks, such as import, play, and organize their music files, video files, photos, and podcasts. Available as a free download from www.apple.com, iTunes also serves as an interface for Apple's portable digital media player, the iPod.

If you connect your computer to the Internet, iTunes serves as a conduit to Apple's iTunes Store, where digital content such as music, audio books, movies, television shows, music videos, and games are available for purchase. You can also access many audio and video podcasts free of charge from the iTunes Store.

Any content that you download or import into iTunes — for example, music files imported from a CD — is accessible from iTunes' Source list, located on the left side of the program window.

Quick Tips

Download iTunes on a PC

Before you can use iTunes on your PC to manage and enjoy your music and other media content, you must first download the program. You do so from a special iTunes download page on Apple's Web site, located at www.apple.com/itunes/download.

The download operation involves stepping through a series of screens in order to specify your preferences for where the iTunes program file should be saved on your computer, as well as whether you want to receive newsletters from Apple.

① Direct your Web browser to www.apple.com/itunes/download.

The Download iTunes page opens.

② Click to select the type of operating system you use (◯ changes to ◉).

● If you want to receive Apple's New Music Tuesday newsletter, select the E-mail me New Music Tuesday check box.

● If you want to receive Apple news, software updates, and information on products and services, select the Keep me up to date check box.

③ Type your e-mail address.

④ Click Download iTunes – Free.

Internet Explorer asks whether you want to run or save the iTunesSetup file.

⑤ Click Run.

● Your computer downloads the iTunes Installer program.

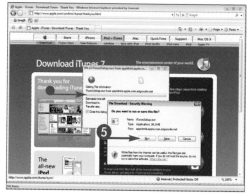

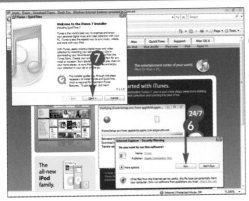

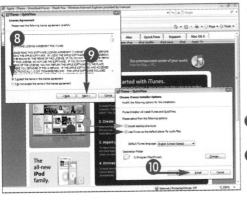

Your Web browser asks whether you want to run iTunes.

6 Click Run.

The iTunes Installer starts.

7 Click Next.

The iTunes Installer displays Apple's license agreement.

8 Click I Accept the Terms in the License Agreement (⚪ changes to ⚫).

9 Click Next.

The Choose iTunes Installer Options screen appears.

● If you want an iTunes shortcut icon to appear on your desktop, select the Install desktop shortcuts check box.

● If you want to use iTunes as the default player for audio files, select the Use iTunes as the default player for audio files check box.

10 Click Install.

The program installs.

11 When the installation is complete, click Finish.

Attention!

From time to time, Apple updates its iTunes software to resolve bugs and add new features. To check whether you have the most recent version of the software, open the iTunes Help menu and select Check for Updates. iTunes checks to see whether you have the most current version; if not, it guides you through the update process. You must be online to check for updates.

Download iTunes on a Mac

If you're using a Mac, you have at least a one-step head start on your Windows-using friends when it comes to iTunes — Apple includes iTunes (and QuickTime) in every version of Mac OS X it distributes. This means that you already have it on your Mac.

If you haven't used iTunes yet, however, there is a strong likelihood that your copy is not the latest and greatest version, since Apple updates iTunes frequently with new features and to ensure compatibility with new hardware (new iPods, AppleTV, the iPhone, etc.). Getting up-to-date, though, is a simple process.

① Click ⬛ (⬛ changes to ⬛).

② Select Software Update.

The Software Update window appears and Mac OS X checks for Apple updates to your software.

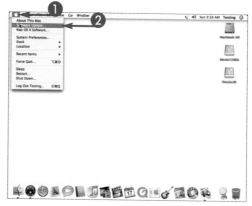

③ Software Update informs you of new versions to your software, including iTunes.

④ Click the Install button to have your new iTunes version downloaded and installed.

Note: Software Update requires that you enter an Administrator password to install a new version and that you accept a Software License Agreement.

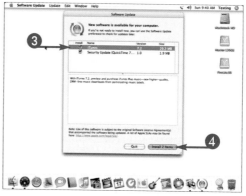

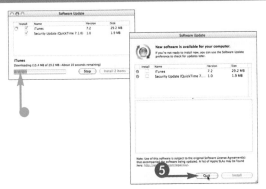

● Software Updates downloads and installs the new iTunes version.

⑤ Click Quit to leave Software Update.

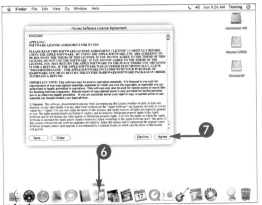

⑥ Click the iTunes icon in the Dock.

iTunes displays Apple's license agreement.

⑦ Click Agree.

Note: If this is the first time you have run iTunes, you are asked a series of questions to set your preferences.

The iTunes window appears.

TIP

Attention!
Apple updates its iTunes software to add new features, support new hardware devices, and fix bugs fairly often. Periodically, click iTunes and then click Check for Updates to ensure that you are up-to-date. iTunes checks to see whether you have the most current version; if not, it guides you through the update process. You must be online to check for updates.

Explore the iTunes Interface

The iTunes interface offers easy access to songs, movies, television shows, podcasts, and audio books saved on your computer.

You can also access Internet radio stations from the iTunes interface, as well as any playlists you have created.

● **View Buttons**
Click one of these buttons to choose a different view setting.

● **Search Field**
To search for iTunes content, type a keyword in the Search field.

● **Source List**
Click a category in the Source list to view music, movies, television shows, podcasts, audio books, or Internet radio stations. You can also access the iTunes Store, view items purchased from the store, and view playlists.

● **File List or Viewer Pane**
After you click a category in the Source list, any files in that category appear here. This pane is also where the iTunes Store appears when selected.

● **Artwork/Video Pane**
View artwork, such as album art, associated with the selected file here.

● **Buttons**
From left to right, click to create a new playlist, shuffle the iTunes content being played, repeat playback of a file or playlist, and show or hide the Artwork/Video pane.

● **Playback Controls**
Click these buttons when enjoying media content on iTunes to skip backward, play or pause, or skip forward in the content. Use the adjacent volume control to adjust the playback volume.

● **Browse Button**
Click here to open a special panel that enables you to browse content by categories such as genre and artist.

● **Menu Bar**
The iTunes menu bar offers access to iTunes commands and options.

● **Eject Button**
Click this button to eject a CD currently in your computer's CD drive.

If you find the regular iTunes window cumbersome, you can collapse it. This collapsed player, called the *MiniPlayer*, features only playback controls, the name of the file being played, and the progress of the playback.

When you collapse the iTunes window to the MiniPlayer, you can set it up to float on top of all other open windows. To do so, open the Edit menu (iTunes on a Mac),

select Preferences, and in the iTunes dialog box that opens, click the Advanced tab. Then click the Keep MiniPlayer on Top of All Other Windows check box to select it. If you prefer to dock the MiniPlayer in your system tray, click the Show iTunes Icon in System Tray and Minimize iTunes Window to System Tray check boxes to select them.

① Click Advanced.

② Click Switch to Mini Player.

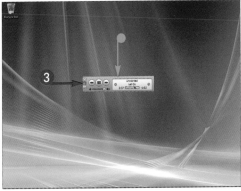

● The iTunes window collapses into the MiniPlayer.

③ To restore the iTunes window to its regular size, click the Restore button (⬜) in the MiniPlayer.

Normalize Volume Settings

If one of your media files is too loud or too soft relative to the others, you can adjust that file's volume setting. To do so, select the file in the File list, click File, and select Get Info. In the dialog box that appears, click the Options tab, drag the Volume Adjustment slider to set the volume, and

click OK. The selected setting applies automatically each time you play that file.

Another option, covered in these steps, is to set up iTunes to play all media files at the same volume level by using iTunes' Sound Check feature.

---

① Click Edit (iTunes on a Mac).

② Click Preferences.

An iTunes dialog box opens.

③ Select the Playback tab.

④ Click the Sound Check check box to select it (changes to ☑).

⑤ Click OK.

iTunes activates Sound Check, analyzes each file in your library to determine its volume levels, and adjusts each file's volume settings as needed.

Over time, you may save thousands of media files on your computer. Fortunately, iTunes offers a few tools for locating files, one of which is its search feature.

Using iTunes' search feature enables you to quickly locate a file in your library or in

a playlist by entering a relevant keyword in the Search field located in the upper-right corner of the iTunes window. You can also use the Search field to find help on using iTunes and your iPod.

① In the Source list, click the category for the type of content you want to find — Music, Movies, TV Shows, Podcasts, or Audiobooks.

Alternatively, you can click a playlist.

② Type a relevant keyword or phrase in the Search field.

iTunes displays a list of files in the selected category or playlist that contain the keyword or phrase you typed.

TIP

Try this!

You can rate the media files that you enjoy by using iTunes' five-star system. You can assign ratings to songs, videos, podcasts, audio books, and any other type of media file supported by iTunes by choosing a number of stars in the My Rating column.

After you've rated your files, you can then sort your media files by rating; just click the My Rating column heading at the top of the File list. (If this column head is not displayed, refer to the task, "Sort Content in iTunes," later in this chapter.) Alternatively, you can use iTunes' Smart Playlist feature to create a playlist containing only those media files to which you have assigned a specified rating.

Browse iTunes for Content

Another tool that iTunes offers for locating files is its Browse feature. Using this feature, you can scan music files in your library by genre, artist, and album, and television episodes by genre, show, and season. iTunes identifies a file's genre, artist, album, and other information from the file's

metadata — that is, information contained within a file about the file. Media files that you purchase from the iTunes Store contain this metadata by default. If no metadata is present in a file, as is often the case with songs imported from CDs, iTunes may be able to obtain the metadata online.

---

① Click the Browse button in the lower-right corner of the iTunes window.

● The iTunes window changes to include multiple panes.

Note: *The names of the panes that display differ, depending on what category of content you select in the Source list — for example, Music, Movies, or TV Shows.*

② Click the genre that you want to browse.

● The contents of the Artist and Album panes change to include only those artists and albums in the genre you chose, and the File list includes only songs in the selected genre.

③ Click the artist you want to browse.

● The contents of the Album pane change to include only albums by the artist you chose, and the contents of the File list include only songs by the selected artist.

Note: *The artist list distinguishes between varied spellings, as well as by presentation. For example, a duet by Tony Bennett and Michael Bublé would not match either artist's name individually.*

④ Click the album you want to browse.

● The contents of the File list change to include only songs in the selected album.

TIP

Try This!
Another way to browse for content is by using iTunes' Cover Flow feature. This feature enables you to browse by cover art, as you might browse a stack of CDs, DVDs, or books. To browse using Cover Flow, click the right-most view button, just to the left of the Search field. Keep in mind that cover art may not be available for all files. Scroll through the cover art by dragging the box in the scroll bar or by clicking the arrows on either side of the scroll bar.

Sort Content in iTunes

An easy way to organize files is to click any one of the column headings in the iTunes window to sort files in the File list. For example, you can sort by name, playing time, artist, and genre. If the criterion by which you want to sort does not appear as a column heading by default, you can add a column that contains the information by which you want to sort.

---

① Click the column heading by which you want to sort.

● iTunes sorts the files in the File list by the column heading you clicked.

Note: To change the sort order from ascending (for example, A to Z) to descending (for example, Z to A), click the column heading a second time. To return to ascending order, click the heading again.

② To add a column by which you want to sort, click View.

③ Click View Options.

The View Options dialog box opens.

④ Select the check box next to the desired column heading or headings (☐ changes to ☑).

This example selects Date Added.

⑤ Click OK.

● The column is added to the File list.

To sort by the new column heading, you can click the heading.

Note: *To quickly jump to an entry in the File list, type the first character in the file's name. iTunes automatically selects the first entry that starts with that character.*

Did You Know?

To move any column, click the column heading and drag it to the new location. To ensure that no single column consumes too much screen space, you can auto-size the columns; that way, they will adjust automatically to the width of their contents. To do so, right-click a column heading and select Auto Size All Columns from the menu that appears.

If you download or import content into iTunes that you later decide you do not want, you can delete it.

When you delete a file from iTunes, you have the option of either completely moving the file to the Recycle Bin (Trash on a Mac) or of simply ensuring that the file will no longer appear in the iTunes File list. Keep in mind that in order to completely delete the file from your system, you must move it

to the Recycle Bin or Trash and then empty the Recycle Bin or Trash.

In addition to deleting individual files, you can also delete folders and playlists from iTunes. When you delete a playlist or a folder, the files within that playlist or folder remain intact. Similarly, you can delete files from within a playlist or folder. Doing so does not remove the file from your library, only from the playlist or folder.

---

① Click to select the file you want to delete.

② Press the Backspace/Delete key.

An iTunes dialog box opens.

● You can click Move to Recycle Bin to move the file to the Recycle Bin.

● You can click Keep Files to keep the file on your computer but to prevent it from displaying in the iTunes File list.

● iTunes removes the file.

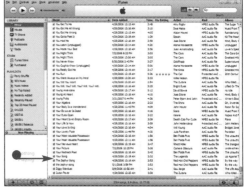

If iTunes or your iPod is not working properly, you can run the program's diagnostic tools to assess the problem. Doing so can help you pinpoint where the problem lies. iTunes also directs you to relevant help topics on Apple's Web site.

When you run iTunes' diagnostic tools, it enables you to specify whether the problem relates to the network, to the CD or DVD drive, or to the iPod.

① Click Help.

② Click Run Diagnostics.

The Diagnostics dialog box opens.

③ Specify whether the problem you want to diagnose relates to the network, to the DVD/CD drive, or to the iPod.

④ Click Next.

iTunes scans to assess the problem and flags any issues it detects.

Remove Duplicate Content

In the event that your library becomes bloated with duplicate content, iTunes makes it easy for you to locate and remove those extra files. Rather than requiring you to scroll through your entire library to locate redundant material, you can instruct iTunes to display all files that contain duplicates. You can then delete the duplicate content just as you would delete any other file: by clicking it in the file list and then clicking the Delete or Backspace key on your keyboard.

---

1 With the library you want to streamline displayed in the iTunes file list (here, the Music library), click View.

2 Click Show Duplicates.

iTunes displays all instances of duplicate files.

3 While holding down the Ctrl key on your keyboard (Cmd key on a Mac), click each instance of a duplicate file.

4 Press the Delete or Backspace key on your keyboard.

iTunes deletes the selected files.

5 To again view your library in its entirety, click Show All.

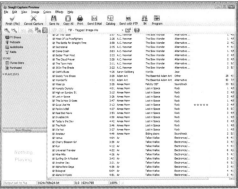

iTunes again displays your library in its entirety.

Attention!

iTunes identifies a file as a duplicate if the file contains the same title and artist as another file. That means if, for example, you have two versions of a song in your library — say, a live version and one recorded in studio — iTunes will flag the files as duplicates, even though they are not. To ensure you do not delete a different version of a song that you want to keep, make it a habit to compare the two files' lengths (in minutes and seconds) before you delete either file.

Although iTunes is intuitive and easy to use, you may still encounter situations in which you need help. In that case, you can use the program's Help function to find the information you need.

BROWSE BY CATEGORY

1 Click Help.

2 Click iTunes Help.

The iTunes Help dialog box opens.

3 Click a category icon to view related articles or subcategories (📁 changes to 📂).

4 If necessary, click a subcategory icon (📁 changes to 📂).

5 When you locate an article that appears relevant, click it.

SEARCH BY KEYWORD

1 Click the Index tab.

2 Type a relevant keyword.

● iTunes' Help locates matching words in the index.

● Articles that relate to the keyword that you typed appear in the Topics Found dialog box.

3 Click the article that seems most relevant.

4 Click Display.

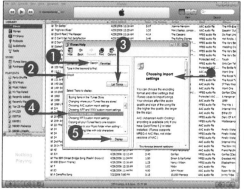

SEARCH BY TOPIC

① Click the Search tab.

② Type a relevant keyword.

③ Click List Topics.

iTunes' Help locates articles that contain the keyword you typed.

④ Click the article that seems most relevant.

⑤ Click Display.

● The contents of the article appear in the right pane.

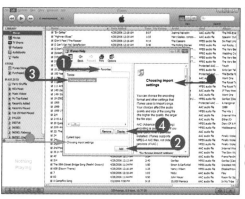

SAVE A HELP ARTICLE AS A FAVORITE

If you frequently search for the same help information, you can save an article as a favorite.

① Click the Favorites tab.

● The name of the article displayed in the right pane appears in the Current Topic field.

② Click Add.

③ To view an article that is added to your favorites, click the article in the Topics area.

④ Click Display.

● The contents of the article appear in the right pane.

More Options!

In addition to offering help information through its Help function, iTunes also offers Hot Tips — tips to help you get more out of iTunes. To access these tips, open the iTunes Help menu and select iTunes Hot Tips. You must be connected to the Internet to access iTunes Hot Tips.

Although Macs and iTunes are easy to use, you might still encounter a situation where you don't know how to accomplish your task. That's where the Mac iTunes Help menu enters the picture. It offers general help for iTunes, the iPod, and

AppleTV; a connection to both the iTunes Service and Support and iPod Service and Support pages (including discussion groups) on Apple's Web site; and a shortcut to a list of all iTunes' keyboard shortcuts.

① Click Help and then iTunes Help.

The Mac Help Viewer opens, displaying the main iTunes Help page.

② Click a topic link to see help information on a topic of interest.

● Click the Index button to see a list of all iTunes-related terms for which Help information can be retrieved.

③ If you have a specific question that none of the links seem to address, type the question into the search box in the top-right portion of the window.

A list of topics, including a ranking for relevancy, appears.

④ When you locate an article that appears relevant, click it.

⑤ Click Show (or double-click the article title) for the contents of the article to appear.

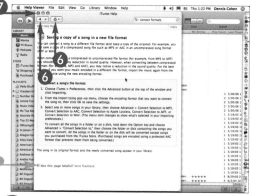

● Click the Send Feedback link at the bottom of an article window if you have comments concerning the page.

⑥ Click the Back button to return to the previous page or the Home button to return to the top-level iTunes Help page.

⑦ To leave Help Viewer, click the window's Close button.

TIP

More Options!

In addition to offering help information through its Help menu, iTunes also offers Hot Tips — tips to help you get more out of iTunes. To access these tips, click the iTunes menu and click iTunes Hot Tips. You must be connected to the Internet to access iTunes Hot Tips. Entries in the iTunes menu take you to the Apple Store for iTunes-related products and to launch your Web browser and send Apple feedback about what you do and don't like or would like to see in a future revision (politeness counts!).

iTunes Store Basics

A great way to build your iTunes library is to obtain content from the iTunes Store. You can find, preview, and purchase songs, albums, videos, television episodes, podcasts, audio books, games, even online classes. You can even purchase some exclusive songs that are available only through the iTunes Store. In addition to the items available for purchase, the iTunes Store also offers some content free of charge – for example, the Store offers a free music single each week, as well as free podcasts and the occasional free television show.

To purchase content from the iTunes Store, you must have an Apple account or an AOL account, as well as a special iTunes Store account. You can pay for purchases you make at the iTunes Store using a credit card, PayPal, or a gift certificate from the iTunes Store. All sales are final.

Your computer must be connected to the Internet in order to visit the iTunes Store (preferably through broadband rather than dial-up).

Quick Tips

Although the iTunes Store is essentially an online storefront, you do not access it with your Web browser as you do other e-commerce sites. Instead, you access the iTunes Store from within the iTunes program installed on your computer.

You can access the iTunes Store from within iTunes in a couple of different ways. One way is to open the Store menu and select Home. Another way is to click the iTunes Store link in the Source list of the iTunes window.

1 In the iTunes window, click iTunes Store in the Source list.

iTunes connects you to the iTunes Store.

Rather than appearing in a separate window, the iTunes Store interface launches in the same iTunes window that you use to manage your own library of media files, replacing the File list. As a result, many of the same controls — including the menus, the playback controls, the Source list, and the Browse

button — remain available in the iTunes Store interface.

In addition to these common screen elements, the iTunes Store home page includes a few of its own elements, including the various links that offer easy access to content, the navigation buttons, and the Search field.

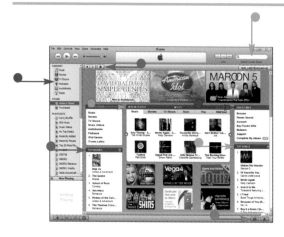

● **Search Field**

To conduct a quick search for content in the iTunes Store, type a relevant keyword in the Search field.

● **Navigation Buttons**

Much like the buttons in a Web browser, you click these navigation buttons to move back to the previous iTunes Store screen, forward to the screen you just moved from, and home – that is, the home page of the iTunes Store.

● **iTunes Store Links**

The links in this section offer quick access to the various iTunes Store categories, including Music, Movies, and TV Shows.

● **Top Movies Links**

This section offers one-click access to the best-selling movies in the iTunes Store.

● **New Releases**

Click the tabs in the New Releases section to access the latest music, movies, and television shows.

● **Top Songs Links**

Use these links to access the top ten most popular songs in the iTunes Store.

● **Quick Links**

Click the links in this section to quickly launch the Browse and Search functions, access your account, buy iTunes gifts, redeem gift certificates, and obtain support.

● **Browse Button**

Click this button to open a special panel that enables you to browse iTunes Store content by categories such as genre and artist.

Although an iTunes account is not required in order to visit the iTunes Store, you need to create an Apple account if you intend to purchase content from the Store.

To set up an Apple account, you must read and agree to Apple's license agreement, and establish a username and password. You must also indicate how you want to pay for any purchases you make at the Store. You can use Visa, MasterCard, American Express, Discover, or PayPal. If you already have an Apple account — for example, if you created an Apple account at the Apple Store Web site or are a .Mac subscriber — you can use the existing account's username and password to log on to the iTunes Store. If you are an AOL user, you can use your AOL username and password to log on to the iTunes Store.

① In the iTunes Store window, click Store.

② Click Create Account.

③ Read the license agreement in the Create an Apple Account for the US iTunes Store screen.

④ Click Agree.

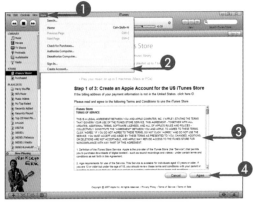

⑤ Type your e-mail address. This serves as your Apple ID.

⑥ Type the password you want to use.

⑦ Retype the password.

⑧ Type a question to confirm your identity if you forget your password.

⑨ Type the answer to the question you entered in Step 8.

⑩ Click the Month and Day and select your birth month and date.

⑪ Click Continue.

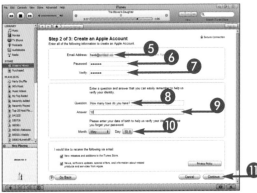

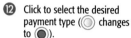

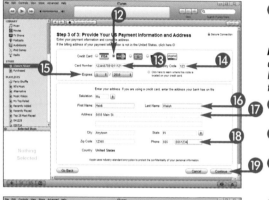

⑫ Click to select the desired payment type (⊙ changes to ◉).

Note: *This example selects a credit card. However, if you choose either the PayPal or None option, simply follow the onscreen prompts.*

⑬ Type the credit card number.

⑭ Type the credit card's security code.

⑮ Using the Expires ⊙, select the card's expiration date (month and year).

⑯ Type your first and last name.

⑰ Type your address.

⑱ Type your phone number.

⑲ Click Continue.

Your Apple account is created.

⑳ Click Done.

TIP

Important!

Depending on your computer's settings, you may be automatically logged in to the iTunes Store when you visit it. If not, you can log on manually. To do so, click the Store menu in the iTunes Store window and select Sign In. In the dialog box that appears, type your Apple ID (that is, the e-mail address you entered in Step 5) and password and click Sign In. To sign out, click the Store menu and then click Sign Out.

If you need to change your account information for the iTunes Store, you can easily do so. For example, if you move, or if your credit card expires, you need to change your address and payment information accordingly.

Alternatively, you can set certain preferences for your account. For example, as outlined in this task, you can enter a nickname. This name appears alongside any iMixes you submit to the iTunes Store. You can also manage your alerts. You can do this by indicating whether the iTunes Store sends you an e-mail message when new content is released from artists whose work you have purchased before.

① In the iTunes Store window, click Store.

② Click View My Account.

③ In the dialog box that opens, type your Apple ID.

④ Type your password.

⑤ Click View Account.

The Apple Account Information screen appears.

● You can click Edit Account Info to change your Apple ID, password, and newsletter-subscription settings.

● You can click Edit Payment Information to change your payment information.

● You can click Manage My Alerts to specify whether the iTunes Store should send you an e-mail message when new content is released from artists whose work you have purchased before.

⑥ Click Create Nickname.

The Create Nickname screen appears.

⑦ Type the nickname you want to use.

⑧ Click Submit.

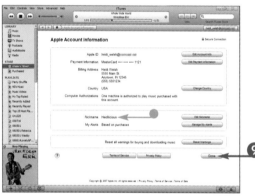

● The nickname you entered is applied to your account.

⑨ Click Done.

The iTunes Store updates your account information.

Important!

You can purchase content from the iTunes Store only if Apple has established an online Store for the country cited in your billing address. As of this writing, Apple supports iTunes Stores in Austria, Belgium, Canada, Finland, France, Germany, Greece, Ireland, Italy, Japan, Luxembourg, the Netherlands, Norway, Portugal, Spain, Sweden, Switzerland, the U.K., and the U.S.

Authorize a Computer to Play iTunes Store Purchases

Before you can use a computer to play content purchased from the iTunes Store, you must authorize that computer. This helps to protect the copyright of certain purchased content. (For a slightly higher price, you can purchase DRM-free music tracks — that is, tracks without digital rights management code embedded — in the iTunes Store, which can be played on any computer.)

You are not limited to authorizing a single computer for playback of content that you purchase from the iTunes Store; in fact, you can authorize as many as five computers. (Your iPod does not require authorization in order to play back content from the iTunes Store.) If you have already authorized five computers, you may not authorize a sixth one unless you first deauthorize one of the original five.

AUTHORIZE A COMPUTER

① Click Store.

② Click Authorize Computer.

The Authorize Computer dialog box appears.

③ Type your Apple ID.

④ Type your password.

⑤ Click Authorize.

The iTunes Store informs you that the authorization was successful.

⑥ Click OK.

DEAUTHORIZE A COMPUTER

1. Click Store.

2. Click Deauthorize Computer.

   The Deauthorize Computer dialog box appears.

3. Type your Apple ID.

4. Type your password.

5. Click OK.

   The iTunes Store informs you that the deauthorization was successful.

6. Click OK.

TIP

Did You Know?

If you fail to deauthorize a computer before selling it or giving it away, you can deauthorize all computers associated with your account at once and then reauthorize those you still use. To do so, click the Store menu, select View My Account, and click the Deauthorize All button. This button is visible only if you have authorized five computers to use your iTunes account. You can execute this operation only once per year.

Restrict Access to Explicit Content

In order to keep consumers informed, the iTunes Store uses labels to indicate content that has been deemed explicit — that is, it contains strong language or depictions of violence, sex, or substance abuse. These labels include Parental Advisory Labels from the Recording Industry Association of America, movie ratings from the Motion Picture Association of America, and television ratings from the TV Parental Guidelines Monitoring Board.

However, if you share your iTunes account with minors, or with others who might find explicit content offensive, you might feel that the use of these labels does not provide adequate protection. In that case, you can restrict access to certain types of content.

① **Click Edit (iTunes on a Mac).**

② **Click Preferences.**

An iTunes dialog box appears.

③ **Click the Parental Control tab (Parental tab on a Mac).**

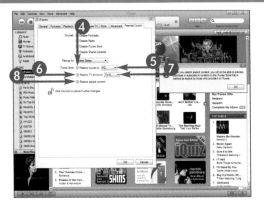

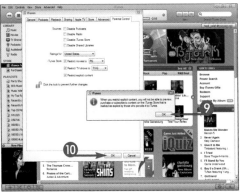

④ To restrict movie content, click the Restrict Movies To check box (changes to ✓).

⑤ To specify the highest acceptable rating level, click here and choose the desired level.

⑥ To restrict television content, click the Restrict TV Shows To check box (changes to ✓).

⑦ To specify the highest acceptable rating level, click here and choose the desired level.

⑧ Click the Restrict Explicit Content check box (changes to ✓).

iTunes warns you that clicking Restrict Explicit Content prevents users from previewing, purchasing, or subscribing to content that is deemed explicit.

⑨ Click OK.

⑩ Click OK.

TIP

More Options!
To ensure that other users cannot change your Parental Control settings, click the Lock icon in the Parental Control tab (Parental on a Mac) of the iTunes dialog box to lock your settings. That way, anyone who attempts to change your settings will be required to enter your Administrator password.

Thanks to the way the iTunes Store is organized, you can browse for content much as you would browse for music at a brick-and-mortar record store or locate a video at your local video-rental outlet.

Content in the iTunes Store is categorized by type: Music, Movies, TV Shows, Music Videos, Audiobooks, Podcasts, and iPod Games. Within each of these categories are multiple subcategories. For example, the Movies category is subdivided into

genres, including Action & Adventure, Comedy, Documentary, Drama, Romance, Sci-Fi & Fantasy, Thriller, and Western, to name a few.

One way to browse is to simply click the various links available in the iTunes Store and see where they take you. However, a more direct approach is to use the Browse feature of the iTunes Store. This feature enables you to pinpoint the content you want with just a few mouse clicks.

① Click the Browse button in the bottom-right corner of the iTunes Store window.

● The iTunes Store window changes to include multiple new panes, with the left-most pane containing a list of the various iTunes Store content categories.

② Click the desired content category.

This example selects Movies.

● A list of movie genres appears in the Genre pane.

Note: *The name and number of panes that display depend on what content category you clicked in Step 2. For example, while clicking the Movies category displays only two panes (iTunes Store and Genre), clicking the Music category displays five panes (iTunes Store, Genre, Subgenre, Artist, and Album).*

③ Click a movie genre.

This example selects Independent.

● The iTunes Store lists available movies in the selected genre.

TIP

Did You Know?
As comprehensive as the iTunes Store's catalog is, it obviously does not include every song, movie, television show, or audio book ever made. If the catalog lacks content that you seek, you can submit a request for Apple to add that content to the catalog. To submit a request, visit the Request Music Web page at www.apple.com/feedback/itunes.html.

Search for Content in the iTunes Store

As of this writing, the iTunes Store catalog featured more than 5,000,000 songs, 100,000 podcasts, 27,000 audio books, and 350 television shows, as well as movies and games. However, as great as it is to have such a wide selection of content, it can also make finding the content you want a bit difficult.

Fortunately, the iTunes Store offers a few tools for locating files, one of which is its Power Search feature. This enables you to enter multiple search parameters, including the content category you want to search, as well as subcategories such as Artist and Genre. The available subcategories differ, depending on what content category you select.

① Click the Power Search link in the Quick Links section of the iTunes Store home page.

A special search screen appears.

② Click the link for the type of content you want to locate.

This example selects Movies.

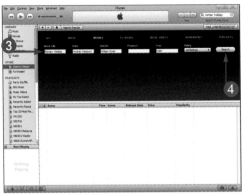

③ In the fields provided, enter information about the item that you seek.

Note: *The available fields differ, according to the type of content for which you are searching.*

④ Click Search.

● iTunes displays the search results, listing entries that match the criteria you entered.

More Options!

An even quicker way to search is to type a keyword or phrase in the Search field in the upper-right corner of the iTunes Store window. When you do this, the iTunes Store displays a list of available items that contain the keyword or phrase you typed. In fact, you might want to use this search method most of the time, and use the Power Search feature only when this method returns an overwhelming number of matches.

Preview Content in the iTunes Store

One of the great things about the iTunes Store is that it enables you to preview the content in its catalog. In the case of songs, the preview lasts 30 seconds, enabling you to determine whether it is indeed the song you want to buy. The same is true for TV show previews. Previews for audio books last 90 seconds, while movie previews are of varying lengths.

When you preview content in iTunes, you may find that playback seems jittery — especially if you have a slow network connection. To rectify this, you can adjust your computer's settings to load the entire preview before playing it. Simply open the Edit menu (iTunes on a Mac), select Preferences, click the Store tab in the iTunes dialog box that appears, click the Load Complete Preview Before Playing check box to select it, and then click OK.

① Locate the content you want to preview, and then click it.

② Click the Play button.

● In this example, because the content is video, the preview appears in the video pane. If the content is audio, you can hear it through your computer's speakers.

③ To view a video preview in a larger window, click the picture in the video pane.

● A larger window opens, displaying the video preview.

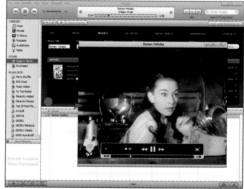

When you purchase content from the iTunes Store, the file containing that content downloads to your computer, where it is saved in your iTunes library and in the Purchased playlist. If the download process is interrupted, it automatically resumes the next time you connect to the iTunes Store, at no extra charge to you. If the download process does not resume automatically, you can open the Store menu, select Check for Purchases, enter your Apple ID and password in the dialog box that appears, and click Check.

If the item you want to purchase has not yet been released, you may be able to pre-order it. When the item becomes available, the iTunes Store notifies you by e-mail; simply click the link in the e-mail to download the item. You are not charged for the item until after you download it.

① After you locate the content you want to preview, click Buy *Content* alongside the content's entry in the list.

● If you no longer want to be prompted for your password, click the Remember Password for Purchasing check box to select it (☐ changes to ☑).

② Type your Apple ID.

③ Type your password.

④ Click Buy.

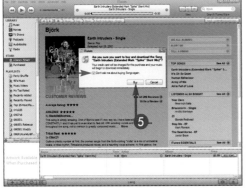

● If you no longer want to be prompted to confirm your purchase of this type of content, you can click the Don't Ask Me about Buying *Content* Again check box to select it (☐ changes to ☑).

⑤ Click Buy.

The file is downloaded to your computer.

Upgrade Your iTunes Store Purchases

Much of the content available through the iTunes Store is protected by Digital Rights Management (DRM). Content that is protected in this manner can be played on computers you have authorized for use with content purchased from the iTunes Store.

Recently, the iTunes Store has begun selling DRM-free music and music video files, called iTunes Plus, which have no usage restrictions, although it may cost a bit more. If your iTunes Library contains DRM-protected content purchased from the iTunes Store that has since been made available as DRM-free content, you can upgrade it.

---

① In the iTunes Store main screen, click iTunes Plus.

iTunes displays the iTunes Plus screen.

② Click See Details.

iTunes displays a list of songs in your library that can be upgraded to iTunes Plus.

③ Click Buy.

iTunes prompts you to decide whether you want to be notified when content is available in DRM-free form.

④ Click iTunes Plus.

iTunes displays the iTunes Store terms and conditions, updated to include information about iTunes Plus.

⑤ Click Accept.

Attention!
You can change iTunes Plus-related account settings from within your iTunes Store Account Information screen. For more information, see the next task.

Initially, all content purchased via the iTunes Store was protected by Digital Rights Management (DRM), meaning it could only be played on authorized computers and faced other restrictions.

Recent developments with content providers has enabled the iTunes Store to offer some content that is free of DRM protection, meaning it has no usage restrictions. Although this content, called iTunes Plus, may cost a bit more, the freedom it provides may prove worth it.

If you want iTunes to notify you when content is available in DRM-free form, thereby giving you the choice to purchase it either with or without the restrictions, you can specify that in your iTunes Store account settings.

① Click Store.

② Click View My Account.

iTunes displays a login dialog box.

③ Enter your Apple ID.

④ Enter your password.

⑤ Click View Account.

The Apple Account Information screen opens.

⑥ Click Manage iTunes Plus.

⑦ Click the Always Show Me iTunes Plus check box to select it.

⑧ Click Save Changes.

● When content is available in iTunes Plus form, iTunes indicates that with a special icon.

Attention!

Currently, only music and music video content is available in DRM-free form. At the time of this writing, DRM-free music files cost $1.29. DRM-free music videos, like their DRM counterparts, cost $1.99.

Shop Using the iTunes MiniStore

The iTunes MiniStore is a small pane that appears at the bottom of your iTunes window. When you play a song, video, or other content in your iTunes library, the MiniStore displays similar items that you might also like – or, barring that, a generic "what's hot today" ad.

If you enjoy receiving music recommendations, you will likely want to enable the display of the MiniStore if it does not display by default. However, if the MiniStore is annoying to you, you can easily turn it off.

① With the contents of your iTunes library displayed in the File list, click View.

② Click Show MiniStore.

● iTunes displays the MiniStore.

③ Click an item in the MiniStore to view it.

● The iTunes Store opens, with the selected item displayed.

You can purchase the item just as you would any other item.

④ To hide the MiniStore, return to your iTunes library by clicking any of the library categories in the Source list.

⑤ Click View.

⑥ Click Hide MiniStore.

iTunes hides the MiniStore.

TIP

Did You Know?

Similar to the iTunes MiniStore, the Just For You feature is also available through the iTunes Store. It introduces you to music that you might enjoy based on your previous purchases. To view your Just For You listings, click the Just For You link, located on the iTunes Store home page.

If you know a person who really loves music, you can set up an iTunes Allowance for them. When you do this, the iTunes Store credits the recipient's account on the first day of each month with the dollar amount you specify, drawing the funds from the credit card or other payment type you set up for your own iTunes Store account. The recipient can then use this credit to purchase music, movies, or other iTunes Store content.

To set up an iTunes Allowance, you need the recipient's Apple ID. If the recipient does not yet have an Apple account, then you need to create one for them.

After you create an iTunes Allowance, the recipient does not need to take any special steps to use it; the recipient's account balance appears alongside their Apple ID in the main iTunes Store window.

① **In the Quick Links section of the iTunes Store home page, click the Buy iTunes Gifts link.**

The Buy iTunes Gifts screen opens.

② **Click the Set up an allowance now link.**

You may need to scroll down to see this option.

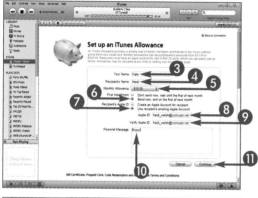

③ Type your name.

④ Type the recipient's name.

⑤ Click the Monthly Allowance ⟨▼⟩ and select the amount you want to deposit each month in the recipient's iTunes Store account.

⑥ Specify whether the first installment should occur now or on the first day of the next month.

⑦ Specify whether you want to create a new Apple account for the recipient or use an existing one.

⑧ Type the recipient's Apple ID.

⑨ Retype the Apple ID.

⑩ Type a message to the recipient.

⑪ Click Continue.

⑫ In the Confirm Your Purchase screen, click Buy.

The iTunes Store sends you an e-mail about the iTunes Allowance and gives you the option of setting up an additional iTunes Allowance.

Important!

You can manage an iTunes Allowance that you have set up. For example, you can change the amount deposited each month, suspend the account, remove the account, or set up a new account. To do this, click the Store menu, select View My Account, and click Manage Allowances in the screen that appears.

Purchase an iTunes Store Gift Certificate

Gift certificates to the iTunes Store make great gifts. Recipients of an iTunes Store gift certificate can use it to purchase anything in the iTunes Store.

The iTunes Store offers three types of gift certificates: gift cards, e-mail gift certificates, or printable gift certificates. When you purchase a gift card from the iTunes Store, the card is sent by mail to the recipient. E-mail gift certificates are immediately sent by e-mail to the

recipient; however, printable gift certificates are printed by the person who purchased the gift for hand delivery. In addition to buying gift cards online, you can also purchase them at many brick-and-mortar stores.

Gift certificates can be used only in the iTunes Store from which they were purchased. For example, if you purchase a gift certificate from the U.S. iTunes Store, it cannot be used in the U.K. iTunes Store.

① In the Quick Links section of the iTunes home page, click the Buy iTunes Gifts link.

The Buy iTunes Gifts screen opens.

② Click the Buy Now link under the desired gift option.

This example selects Email Gift Certificates.

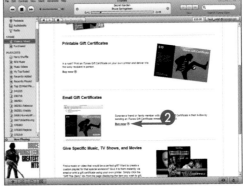

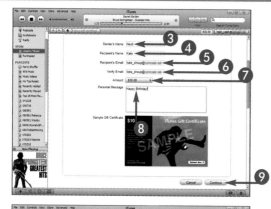

③ Type your name.

④ Type the recipient's name.

⑤ Type the recipient's e-mail address.

This does not need to match the recipient's Apple ID. Any working e-mail address will do.

⑥ Retype the e-mail address.

⑦ Click the Amount 🔽 and select a dollar amount for the gift certificate.

⑧ Type a message to the recipient.

⑨ Click Continue.

Note: If you are prompted, type your Apple ID and password and click Setup.

⑩ In the Confirm Your Purchase screen, click Buy.

The iTunes Store sends an e-mail containing the gift certificate to the recipient and gives you the option of buying another gift certificate. To do so, click Buy Another; otherwise, click Done.

More Options!

In addition to giving gift certificates through the iTunes Store, you can also give specific songs, albums, movies, audio books, and other content. To do so, simply display the item you want to give on its own page, click the Gift This link alongside the item, and follow the onscreen instructions.

Redeem an iTunes Gift Certificate

If you receive a gift certificate from someone, you must redeem it in order to use it to purchase items from the iTunes Store. The process for redeeming the gift certificate is essentially the same, regardless of whether it was e-mailed to you, is a printout, a gift card, or a promotional code that you received from an iTunes Store partner.

Any gift certificate that you receive can be used only in the iTunes Store from which it was purchased. For example, if your gift certificate was purchased from the U.S. iTunes Store, it cannot be used in the U.K. iTunes Store.

① In the Quick Links section of the iTunes home page, click the Redeem link.

② Type the code found on the iTunes Store gift certificate, gift card, or promotional coupon.

③ Click Redeem.

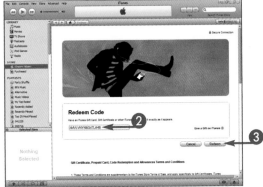

An iTunes dialog box appears, asking you to confirm that you want to redeem your gift certificate.

④ Click Redeem Gift Certificate.

⑤ Click Done.

● The balance of your iTunes Store account appears next to your Apple ID in the iTunes Store window.

Apply It!

If you received your gift certificate through e-mail, you can redeem it by clicking the Redeem Now button in the body of the e-mail message. Doing so launches the iTunes Store, with the iTunes dialog box displayed. Click Gift Certificate. The iTunes Store confirms that the gift certificate has been redeemed, and the amount added to your account appears next to your Apple ID in the iTunes window. Click Done.

Get iTunes Store Support

Although the iTunes Store is intuitive and easy to use, you may still encounter situations in which you need help. In that case, you can use the Support features to find the information you need or to obtain program support.

The iTunes Store offers support through a special Web site, where you can find links to customer support and frequently asked questions.

---

① Click the Support link in the Quick Links section of the iTunes Store home page.

iTunes launches your Web browser, and the iTunes Store help page displays.

● To search for help, type a keyword in the Search Support field.

● The Customer Service area includes links to helpful articles relating to customer service.

- The User Discussions section offers links to customer forums.

- The Troubleshooting section includes links to Apple articles about troubleshooting the iTunes Store.

② Click a link on the Web page to view the associated article.

- The associated article opens.

Important!

If you cannot connect to the iTunes Store, the problem may be your Internet connection. Try launching your Web browser and connecting to a different site. If you can connect, then you know the problem is not the Internet connection; in that case, the problem may be with the iTunes Store, in which case your best option may be to simply visit the Store at another time.

55

iPod Basics

When Apple introduced the iPod in October of 2001, it made it possible for music lovers everywhere to store their song collections on a device that fit in the palm of their hand, and to listen to that collection while on the go.

Not content to stop there, Apple expanded the iPod's capabilities to store and display video. Indeed, the current generation of iPods can store as much as 80GB of content — which means it can hold as many as 20,000 songs, 25,000 photos, 100 hours of video, or any combination thereof. The device's vibrant display makes viewing this content a pleasure, and its extended battery life — 20 hours of audio or 6 hours of video — ensures that your iPod does not run out of charge at a climactic moment.

In addition to offering these media features, an iPod can also serve as a personal digital assistant, storing your contacts and calendar entries, as well as enabling you to set alarms and keep notes. You can even enable the iPod to store data files from your computer, as well as use the device to play games.

Quick Tips

Your iPod features intuitive controls that make it possible for you to enjoy your music, videos, and other content with a minimal learning curve. It features a button that doubles as Play and Pause control, a Previous/Rewind button, and a Next/Fast Forward button. A fourth button, labeled Menu, offers quick access to the iPod's menu system.

The iPod's click wheel enables you to both navigate the iPod menus and adjust the volume setting, and the Select button is used to select menu items.

● **Previous/ Rewind Button**
Press this button once to return to the beginning of the current song, or multiple times to return to a previous song. To rewind through a song, hold the button down.

● **Menu Button**
Press this button to move upward through the menus.

● **Play/Pause Button**
Press this button once to play the currently selected media file. To pause playback, press it again.

● **Dock Connector**
Insert the cable that accompanied your iPod here to connect it to your computer.

● **Hold Switch**
When the Hold switch is turned on, all iPod buttons and settings are locked.

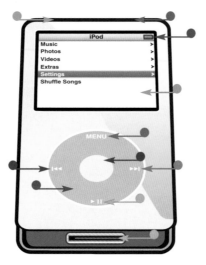

● **Click Wheel**
Touch the click wheel and drag clockwise to navigate down a menu list or counter-clockwise to navigate up the list. You can also use the click wheel to increase or decrease volume during playback.

● **Headphone Jack**
Insert your headphones here.

● **Battery Charge Indicator**
This screen icon indicates the status of the battery charge.

● **iPod Screen**
The iPod screen displays when the iPod is powered on.

● **Next/Fast Forward Button**
Press this button once to skip to the beginning of the next song, or multiple times to skip to subsequent songs in the list. To fast-forward through a song, hold the button down.

● **Select Button**
Press this button to select a menu item or to move downward through the menus.

Understanding the iPod Menus

Chapter 3

Starting with the iPod menu, the iPod presents many menus. You make selections on the menu using the click wheel to scroll up and down. To select a menu or option, press the Select button in the middle of the click wheel.

Because of the iPod's relatively small screen, only a limited number of menu items can appear at once. When there are more menu options than can display at once, a scroll bar appears; to see the additional selections, touch the click wheel and drag clockwise until you reach the bottom of the menu.

● **iPod Menu**
The iPod menu, which is the top menu in the iPod, displays automatically whenever you power on your iPod.

● **Music Menu**
The iPod's Music menu acts as a gateway to the music stored on the device. You can browse your collection using various criteria, such as artists, songs, and genres.

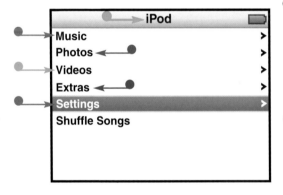

● **Photos Menu**
To view photos stored on your iPod, select the Photos menu. This menu also provides access to settings that you can establish to display your photos in a slide show.

● **Videos Menu**
Opening the Videos menu enables you to access movies, music videos, and podcasts. You can also access video settings from this menu.

● **Settings Menu**
In addition to enabling you to view information about your iPod, the Settings menu offers access to tools that enable you to customize your iPod. These include Volume Limit, Backlight Timer, Brightness, EQ, and Date & Time.

● **Extras Menu**
To access iPod features not related to music, video, or photos – including the clock, games, contacts, calendar entries, notes, stopwatch, or Screen Lock feature – open the Extras menu.

59

When you connect your iPod to your computer, new content and playlists in your iTunes are copied to the iPod, and any content that has been deleted from iTunes is removed from the iPod — a process called *syncing*. You can also *reverse sync* — that is, sync items you have purchased from the iTunes Store that are on your iPod to another authorized computer. You can disable this automatic synchronization, opting instead to manually sync your iPod.

Regardless of whether you synchronize manually or automatically, do not disconnect your iPod from your computer during the sync process. Otherwise, you may damage the data on your iPod. After the sync operation is complete, click the Eject button alongside the iPod entry in the iTunes Source list, and then extract the cable from your iPod.

DISABLE AUTOMATIC SYNCING

1 Attach your iPod to your computer using the cable provided.

iTunes starts, displaying a special iPod screen.

2 Click the Manually Manage Music and Videos check box (changes to ✓).

3 Click Apply.

iTunes asks you to confirm that you want to manually manage your music and videos, and indicates that you need to manually eject your iPod in order to disconnect it safely.

4 Click OK.

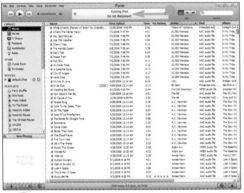

MANUALLY SYNC YOUR IPOD

1️⃣ Attach your iPod to your computer using the cable provided.

iTunes starts.

2️⃣ Click File.

3️⃣ Click Sync iPod.

If you want to transfer purchased content that resides on your iPod to another authorized computer, you can choose Transfer Purchases from iPod from the File menu.

● iTunes syncs your iPod.

Important!
By default, iTunes syncs your iPod to reflect all content changes since the last sync operation. To sync only selected items, connect your iPod to your computer and click the iPod entry in the iTunes Source list. In the screen that appears, click a content-type tab and choose the desired sync options. You might choose to sync only certain items if, for example, your iPod is near capacity.

Suppose you want to download a movie file to your iPod, but you are not certain you have adequate space on the device's hard drive. Fortunately, Apple makes it easy to determine how much space is available on your iPod — although you must do so through iTunes.

Your iPod must be connected to your computer in order for you to be able to assess disk space.

① Connect your iPod to your computer.

② In the Source list, click the iPod entry.

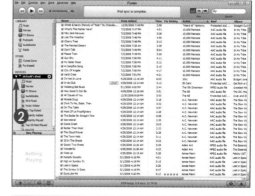

The iPod Summary screen appears.

● You can view available space here.

Although the current generation of iPods can store as much as 80GB of content, it is possible that your iPod might run out of space for new content. If you find your iPod is becoming full, preventing you from adding new content, you can delete items from the device.

To do so, you must first disable automatic syncing; that way, iTunes does not attempt to add new content to your iPod each time you connect the device to your computer. After you disable automatic syncing, you can delete any content that you no longer use from your iPod. For more information on disabling automatic syncing, see the task "Sync Your iPod with iTunes."

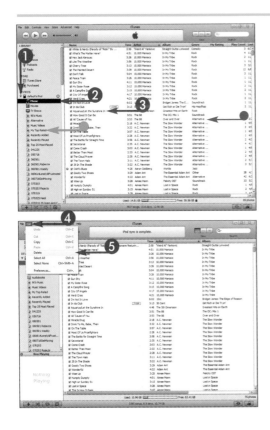

① After connecting your iPod to your computer and disabling automatic syncing, click the ▶ next to the iPod entry in the Source list (▶ changes to ▼).

● iTunes displays a list of content in your iPod.

② Click the category of the content you want to delete.

● iTunes displays the available content in the selected category.

③ Click an item you want to delete.

④ Click Edit.

⑤ Click Delete.

iTunes deletes the item from your iPod.

Browse for Content on Your iPod

As great as it is to be able to store so many songs, photos, and hours of video on your iPod, actually finding the file you want to play can be like finding a needle in a haystack.

Fortunately, iPods are designed to help you easily find the content you want. One way is by including an intuitive menu system, which divides content into several categories. These include Music, Photos, Videos, and Extras. Selecting any one of these menu entries launches a series of submenus, which you in turn select to tunnel down to the content you seek.

① In the main iPod screen, use the click wheel to highlight a menu item.

This example selects Music.

Note: If the iPod screen is not currently displayed, you can press the Menu button on your iPod as many times as needed to reveal it.

② Press the Select button.

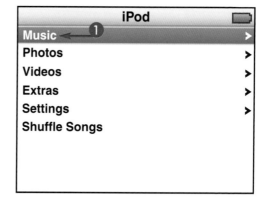

The contents of the Music menu appear.

③ Using your click wheel, scroll to the desired menu item.

This example selects Artists.

④ Press the Select button.

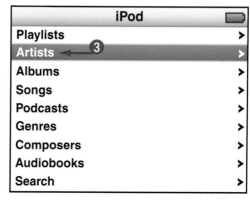

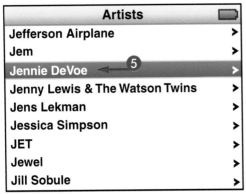

Your iPod displays a list of the artists represented in your music catalog.

5 Using your click wheel, scroll to the desired artist.

6 Press the Select button.

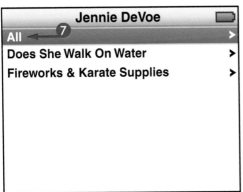

Songs or albums by the selected artist appear on your iPod's screen.

7 Using your click wheel, scroll to the song or album you want to hear.

Alternatively, you can choose All.

8 Press the Play button.

iPod plays back the song or album you selected.

Did You Know?
By default, your iPod emits a quiet clicking noise as you scroll through the various menus with the click wheel. This helps you gauge how quickly you are scrolling. If you prefer to scroll silently, you can disable this clicking feature. To do so, select Settings in the main iPod screen. Then, in the screen that appears, select Clicker.

Search for Content on Your iPod

Although the iPod's menu system is designed to be intuitive and easy to use, you may find that actually locating your files — especially music files — can require a few more steps than you would like. A quicker method might be to search for content. When you opt to search for a music file, your iPod's screen changes to include a keyboard; you can use the device's click wheel and Select button to scroll to and select each letter in the keyword by which you want to search.

Keep in mind that an iPod can search only for audio content; it does not support searching for other types of files, such as video files.

---

① In the main iPod screen, use the click wheel to highlight the Music menu item.

② Press the Select button.

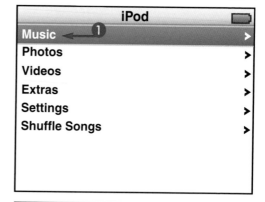

The contents of the Music menu appear.

③ Using your click wheel, scroll to the Search menu item.

④ Press the Select button.

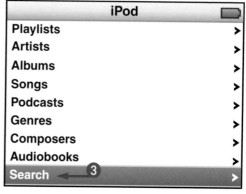

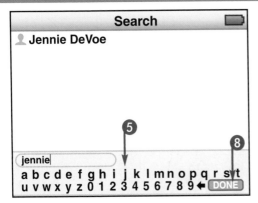

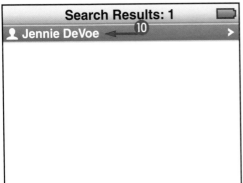

⑤ Using your click wheel, scroll to the first letter of the keyword by which you want to search.

⑥ Press the Select button.

⑦ Repeat Steps 5 and 6 until the desired item appears in the list of matches.

⑧ Using your click wheel, scroll to the Done option.

⑨ Press the Select button.

⑩ If necessary, use your click wheel to scroll to the desired match in the Search Results screen.

⑪ Press the Select button.

⑫ Press the Play button.

The iPod plays back the selected item.

Important!
If you type a letter or number by accident while entering your search word or phrase, you can erase it by clicking the Previous/Rewind button or by scrolling to the left-pointing arrow next to the Done entry. To enter a space in the keyword or phrase, press the Next/Fast Forward button.

Customize Your iPod's Main Menu

If you frequently access a setting or option that is embedded deep in your iPod's menu structure, you can add that setting or option to the main iPod menu. That way, instead of navigating through multiple screens to access the setting, you can quickly select the option or setting from the main iPod screen.

Of course, if you change your mind about adding an item to the main iPod screen, you can easily remove it. In fact, you can remove all items that you have added to the main iPod screen in one operation: Reset Main Menu.

---

① In the main iPod screen, use the click wheel to highlight the Settings menu item.

② Press the Select button.

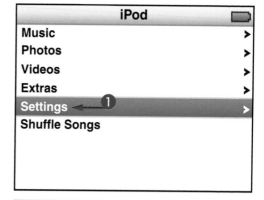

The Settings screen appears.

③ Using your click wheel, scroll to the Main Menu option.

④ Press the Select button.

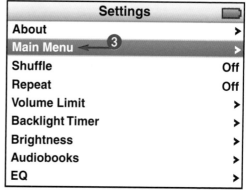

Main Menu	🔋
Videos	On
Extras	On
Clock	Off
Stopwatch ← ⑤	Off
Screen Lock	Off
Contacts	Off
Calendar	Off
Notes	Off
Voice Memos	Off

iPod	🔋
Music	›
Photos	›
Videos	›
Extras	›
Stopwatch ←	›
Settings	›
Shuffle Songs	›

The Main Menu screen appears.

⑤ Using your click wheel, scroll to the entry for the option or setting you want to add to the main iPod screen (the selected item's Off status changes to On).

This example selects Stopwatch.

⑥ Press the Select button.

⑦ Press the Menu button as many times as needed to return to the main iPod screen.

● The option or setting you selected appears in the main iPod screen.

TIP

Did You Know?
If, after adding an item to the main iPod screen, you want to remove it, you can easily do so. Simply repeat the steps in this task, so that the item's On status changes to Off. Alternatively, you can reset the main iPod screen to its original state by choosing Reset Main Menu in the Main Menu screen; then, when prompted, choose Reset.

69

Adjust iPod Sound and Volume Settings

One way to adjust volume on your iPod is to drag a finger around the click wheel, moving clockwise to increase volume and counter-clockwise to decrease it.

Adjusting volume in this way changes the volume for files that you are playing, but it does not account for the fact that certain songs or videos may have been recorded at different levels, making them louder or softer. You can set up your iPod to play all your media files at the same volume level by using iTunes' Sound Check feature.

In addition to using Sound Check, you can also use your iPod's EQ function to fine-tune your sound. The iPod's EQ function includes more than 20 pre-set configurations from which to choose, many of which are designed for specific genres.

ENABLE SOUND CHECK

① In the main iPod screen, use the click wheel to highlight the Settings menu item.

② Press the Select button.

The Settings screen appears.

③ Using your click wheel, scroll to the Sound Check option.

④ Press the Select button.

Your iPod activates Sound Check, analyzing each file stored on the device to determine its volume levels and adjusting each file's volume settings as needed.

⑤ Press the Menu button as many times as needed to return to the main iPod screen.

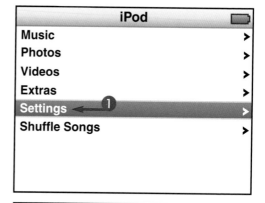

iPod

Music ➤
Photos ➤
Videos ➤
Extras ➤
Settings ← ① ➤
Shuffle Songs ➤

Settings

Backlight Timer ➤
Brightness ➤
Audiobooks ➤
EQ ➤
Compiling ➤
Sound Check ← ③ ➤
Clicker ➤
Date & Time ➤
Contacts ➤

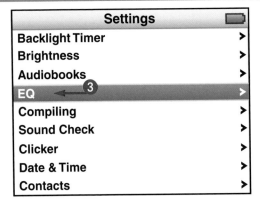

Settings	
Backlight Timer	>
Brightness	>
Audiobooks	>
EQ	>
Compiling	>
Sound Check	>
Clicker	>
Date & Time	>
Contacts	>

EQ	
Jazz	>
Latin	>
Loudness	>
Lounge	>
Piano	>
Pop	>
R & B	>
Rock	>
Small Speakers	>

CHOOSE AN EQ PRE-SET

① In the main iPod screen, use the click wheel to highlight the Settings menu item.

② Press the Select button.

The Settings screen appears.

③ Using your click wheel, scroll to the EQ option.

④ Press the Select button.

The EQ screen appears.

⑤ Using your click wheel, scroll to the desired EQ pre-set.

⑥ Press the Select button.

The selected EQ pre-set is applied.

⑦ Press the Menu button as many times as needed to return to the main iPod screen.

Did You Know?

To protect your ears, you can set a volume limit. To do so, choose Settings in the main iPod screen. Then choose Volume Limit, use the click wheel to drag the slider to the left or right to lower or raise the limit respectively, and press the Select button. Optionally, you can lock in the volume limit by choosing Set Combination and using the click wheel and the Select button to enter a combination.

Adjust iPod Video Settings

The current generation of iPods can store as many as 100 hours of video — meaning that it also has a screen that is of sufficient quality to display video. Although the iPod's screen is small – 2.5 inches, to be precise — it is surprisingly vibrant, resulting in a pleasurable (if not immersive) viewing experience.

To customize the screen display, you can adjust various video settings on your iPod, such as the aspect ratio (that is, whether video displays in widescreen format) and how bright the screen is.

Keep in mind that if you increase the screen's brightness, the amount of time your iPod can play before being recharged is reduced.

CHANGE THE ASPECT RATIO

① In the main iPod screen, use the click wheel to highlight the Videos menu item.

If the iPod screen is not currently displayed, you can press the Menu button on your iPod as many times as needed to reveal it.

② Press the Select button.

The Videos screen appears.

③ Using your click wheel, scroll to the Video Settings option.

④ Press the Select button.

The Settings screen appears.

⑤ Using your click wheel, scroll to the Widescreen option.

⑥ Press the Select button (Off changes to On, or vice versa, depending on the original setting).

⑦ Press the Menu button as many times as needed to return to the main iPod screen.

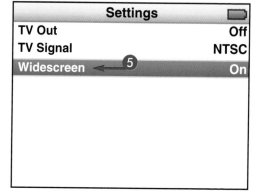

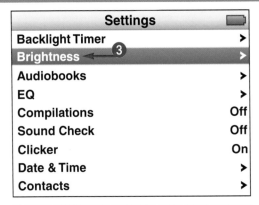

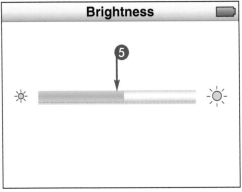

CHANGE BRIGHTNESS SETTINGS

1 In the main iPod screen, use the click wheel to highlight the Settings menu item.

If the iPod screen is not currently displayed, you can press the Menu button on your iPod as many times as needed to reveal it.

2 Press the Select button.

The Settings screen appears.

3 Using your click wheel, scroll to the Brightness option.

4 Press the Select button.

The Brightness screen appears.

5 Using your click wheel, drag the slider to the left or right to reduce or increase the brightness level, respectively.

6 Press the Select button.

The iPod applies the selected changes.

7 Press the Menu button as many times as needed to return to the main iPod screen.

Did You Know?

If you are unhappy with the brightness levels as you view a video, you can adjust them without stopping playback. To do so, press the Select button twice; this displays the Brightness slider. Use your click wheel to drag the slider to the left or right; when the screen's brightness is to your liking, press the Select button a third time to set it.

By default, the music in your iPod displays alphabetically by artist, song, genre, and other categories. For example, if you were to choose Songs from the Music screen, you would see all the songs stored in your iPod in alphabetical order.

If you want to play back content in a random, rather than alphabetical, order,

you can *shuffle* it. For example, you can choose to shuffle by song, so that any song in your library is eligible for playback in random order, or by album, meaning that you hear an entire album before the next album is randomly selected for play.

① In the main iPod screen, use the click wheel to highlight the Settings menu item.

② Press the Select button.

The Settings screen appears.

③ Using your click wheel, scroll to the Shuffle option.

④ Press the Select button.

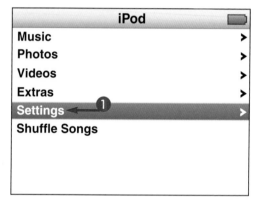

The Shuffle setting changes to Off, Songs, or Albums, depending on the original setting.

⑤ Press the Menu button as many times as needed to return to the main iPod screen.

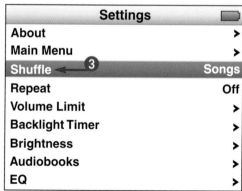

Suppose you are trying to decipher the lyrics of a song. Or maybe you just obtained a new track that you really enjoy. Rather than pressing the Previous/Rewind button on your iPod at the end of the song to restart the song over and over again, you can enable your iPod's Repeat feature. This feature enables you to listen to the same song as many times as you like, without touching the click wheel.

In addition to enabling you to repeat playback of a single song, the Repeat feature can be used to repeat playback of a playlist or your entire music library.

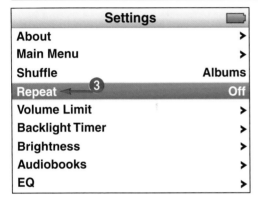

① In the main iPod screen, use the click wheel to highlight the Settings menu item.

② Press the Select button.

   The Settings screen appears.

③ Using your click wheel, scroll to the Repeat option.

④ Press the Select button.

● The Repeat setting changes to Off, One, or All, depending on the original setting.

⑤ Press the Menu button as many times as needed to return to the main iPod screen.

Although Apple is an American company, it has wisely designed its iPod for international use. To this end, you can customize your iPod to display the names of menus and screens in any one of several different languages. Available languages include Chinese, Dutch, French, German, Italian, Japanese, Korean, Polish, Portuguese, Spanish, Swedish, and Turkish, to name a few. Note that changing the iPod's language settings does not affect the language in which your content displays.

In addition to changing the language settings on your iPod, you can also change language settings in iTunes, which has the same languages available as the iPod. When you change the iTunes language settings, any menus or other screen elements feature the language you selected.

① In the main iPod screen, use the click wheel to highlight the Settings menu item.

② Press the Select button.

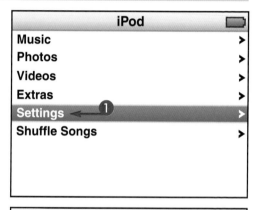

The Settings screen appears.

③ Using your click wheel, scroll to the Language option.

④ Press the Select button.

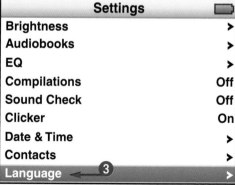

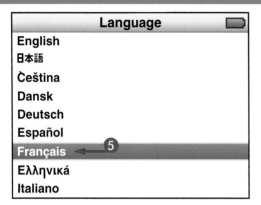

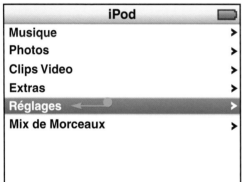

The Language screen appears.

⑤ Scroll to the language you want your iPod to display.

⑥ Press the Select button.

⑦ Press the Menu button as many times as needed to return to the main iPod screen.

● The menu commands now appear in the language you selected.

Did You Know?

If you have changed the language settings on your iPod, chances are you also want to change them in iTunes. To do so, open the Edit menu and choose Preferences (iTunes and Preferences on the Mac). In the General tab of the dialog box that appears, click the Language ☑ and choose the desired language from the menu that appears. Click OK and then restart iTunes to implement the change.

To prevent others from using your iPod, you can enable Screen Lock. When the screen is locked, your iPod continues doing whatever it was doing before you locked it. For example, if your iPod was playing music, it continues to do so. Although you can pause and resume playback even when the screen is locked, you cannot adjust the volume or change what content is playing.

The first time you enable Screen Lock, your iPod prompts you to establish a four-digit combination, with which you can unlock the screen. Use your click wheel to choose the first number and then press the Select button; then repeat these steps to set the remaining three numbers.

Alternatively, you can connect the iPod to your computer; when you disconnect it, the iPod screen is no longer locked.

① In the main iPod screen, use the click wheel to highlight the Extras menu item.

② Press the Select button.

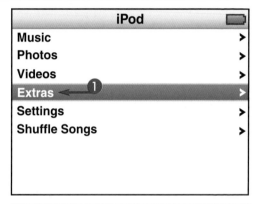

The Extras screen appears.

③ Using your click wheel, scroll to the Screen Lock option.

④ Press the Select button.

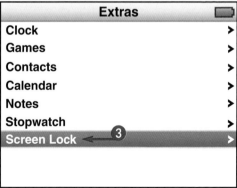

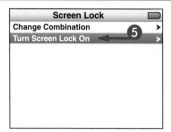

The Screen Lock screen appears.

⑤ Choose Turn Screen Lock On.

⑥ Press the Select button.

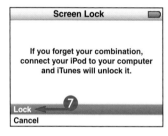

Your iPod informs you that if you forget your combination, you should connect your iPod to your computer to unlock the screen.

⑦ Choose Lock.

⑧ Press the Select button.

The iPod screen is now locked.

⑨ To unlock the iPod screen, enter the four-digit combination, using your click wheel and the Select button to choose each number.

⑩ Press Select once more.

⑪ Press the Menu button as many times as needed to return to the main iPod screen.

Caution!

If you forget your combination, and you do not have access to the primary computer used for your iPod, your only option is to *restore* the iPod to its factory settings — an operation that erases all contents from the device. To do so, connect the iPod to a computer, select the iPod from the Source list, and click the Restore button in iTunes' iPod Summary screen.

Although your iPod is designed to be intuitive and easy to use, you may still encounter situations in which you need help with it. Unfortunately, there is no help function installed on the iPod, meaning if you run into a problem while on the go, you cannot troubleshoot using the iPod as your help resource. However, you can access iPod help from within

iTunes. When you do, you are directed to a screen that enables you to access different areas of Apple's Web site, where you can find links to articles and tutorials.

Note that you must be connected to the Internet in order to access iPod's help information, but your iPod does not need to be connected to your computer.

① In the iTunes window, click Help.

② Click iPod Help.

The iPod Help dialog box opens.

③ Click any of the iPod Help links.

This example selects Tutorials.

Your Web browser automatically launches, and goes to the page associated with the link that you clicked in Step 3.

④ Click a link on the page to view the associated help information.

The precise steps you take to access help information on Apple's Web site may vary. For example, if you want to view a video tutorial, you must click the video window to play the tutorial. Simply follow the onscreen instructions.

● The help information displays.

More Options

If you need to access Apple's support resources for your iPod, open the Help menu in iTunes and choose iPod Service and Support. This launches your Web browser and directs it to Apple's support Web page for iPods. There you can find help articles, troubleshooting information, discussion groups, and other iPod help resources.

Enjoy Music with iTunes and Your iPod

Although iTunes and the iPod have evolved since their introduction in 2001 to support playback of video and other types of content, both were originally audio-only. It is therefore no surprise that both iTunes and the iPod support a wide range of audio features and activities.

Using iTunes, you can play music files stored on your computer as well as play CDs that you insert in your computer's CD drive. You can import these files into your iTunes library, converting them to iTunes' proprietary format. You can also use the program to find information about songs on a CD, as well as to enter and view lyrics. Using iTunes' program settings, you can customize your listening experience — enabling Visualizer effects and fading songs in and out.

In addition to using iTunes to enjoy your music, you can also play back your music on your iPod. Indeed, the iPod provides you with access to your entire music library while you are on the go — on a device that fits snugly in the palm of your hand.

Quick Tips

Add a Song on Your Computer to iTunes

If you have already copied music files or other types of audio files to your computer prior to downloading iTunes, you can easily add those files to your iTunes library. Doing so creates a copy of the file in a format that you can play back in iTunes and on your iPod.

One way to add music files to your iTunes library is to do so one file at a time, as

described here. Alternatively, you can add all audio files contained within a particular folder to your iTunes library. Either way, the original version of each file remains intact in the original location, with a copy of the file in its new format saved in the iTunes folder.

① Click File.

② Click Add File to Library.

The Add To Library dialog box appears.

Note: *The look and feel of this dialog box differs depending on what operating system you use.*

③ Locate and click the file you want to add.

④ Click Open.

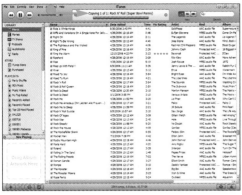

● iTunes adds the file, showing you the progress of the operation as it does.

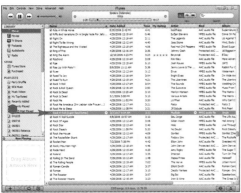

● The file is listed in your library.

More Options

In addition to adding files on your computer to iTunes one at a time, you can also add the audio contents of an entire folder to your iTunes library. To do so, click File, choose Add Folder to Library, locate and select the folder that contains the audio you want to add, and click OK. Alternatively, drag the folder from Windows Explorer or the Mac Finder onto the Music entry in the source list.

Add a Song on the Internet to iTunes

As discussed in Chapter 2, one way to obtain songs online is to purchase them from the iTunes Store. However, that is not the only method by which you can obtain music online for playback in iTunes. Music is available for download on many sites on the Internet, sometimes free of charge and other times for a fee.

The first step is to download music from the Internet to your computer's hard

drive. From there, you can add the song to the iTunes library. Keep in mind that the steps for downloading a file from the Internet are different, depending on whether your computer is a Mac or a PC, as well as which browser you use and the security settings you have established for that browser. The example downloads a file to a PC.

① When you find a song online that you want to download, take the necessary steps to do so.

The precise steps for downloading music from the Internet vary from site to site. For guidance, you can visit the site's help pages.

The File Download dialog box appears.

② Click Save.

The Save As dialog box opens.

③ Locate and select the folder in which you want to save the downloaded music file.

④ If necessary, type a name for the music file.

⑤ Click Save.

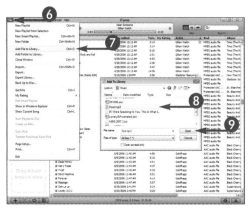

6 Click File.

7 Click Add File to Library.

The Add To Library dialog box appears.

8 Locate and click the file you just downloaded.

9 Click Open.

● The file is listed in your library.

Caution!

Be certain that you have permission to download a song from the Internet before you do so. Otherwise, downloading music from the Web is considered stealing — a matter that record companies and others in the music industry take very seriously. If you purchase a song from an online music store or download a song directly from an artist's or record label's site, you can reasonably assume that permission has been granted.

Import CDs into iTunes

You probably have a collection of CDs that you have built over a period of years or perhaps even decades. You can import the songs on those CDs into iTunes, meaning that you can listen to them from the iTunes program or on your iPod without inserting the CD into your computer's CD drive.

When you *import* a song from a CD into iTunes, you store a copy of the song file on your hard drive. This file is saved in the Advanced Audio Coding (AAC) file format, which compresses song files so that they do not consume a large amount of disk space.

If you want iTunes to automatically obtain information about the tracks you import, such as their name and the artist, you must import songs while connected to the Internet.

① **With iTunes open, insert the CD containing the songs you want to import in your computer's CD drive.**

● The name of the CD displays in the Source list.

● The contents of the CD display in the File list.

② **Click the check box next to any song that you do not want to import (☑ changes to ☐).**

③ **Click Import CD.**

iTunes imports the selected songs on the CD.

● The song currently being imported is marked with ⊘.

● Songs for which the import operation is complete are marked with ✔.

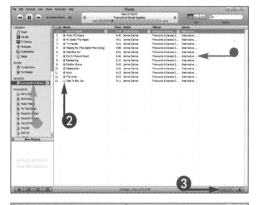

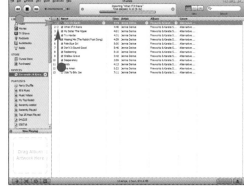

When all of the songs have been imported, iTunes alerts you with an audible signal.

④ Click Music in the Source list.

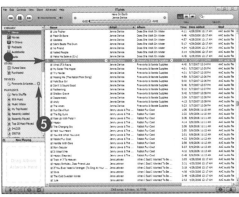

● The songs you imported are now available from the File list.

⑤ To eject the CD, click ⏏ next to the CD's name in the Source list.

Did You Know?

If, after importing songs from a CD, you discover that they do not sound right — for example, if you hear popping or clicking noises — then it may be that the CD drive on your computer failed to read the disc correctly. To rectify this, try enabling iTunes' Error Correction feature. Open the Edit menu (iTunes on a Mac), click Preferences, click Advanced, click Importing, and then click the Use Error Correction When Reading Audio CDs check box to select it.

Change Import Settings

By default, when you import a song into iTunes, it is encoded in the Advanced Audio Coding (AAC) file format. This format compresses song files so that they do not consume a large amount of disk space. Nonetheless, you might prefer that imported files be encoded in a different format — for example, in MP3 format —

so that you can play them on a music player other than an iPod. You can change this and other import settings, such as bit rate.

In this context, *bit rate* describes the number of kilobits per second of audio in an audio file. Higher bit rates result in larger files, but also higher-quality files.

① Click Edit (iTunes on a Mac)

② Click Preferences.

An iTunes dialog box appears.

③ Click the Advanced tab.

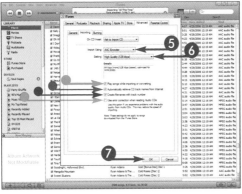

④ Click the Importing tab.

⑤ Click the Import Using ▾ and choose the desired type of encoder.

The encoder is the utility that iTunes uses to encode the file in a different format, such as MP3.

⑥ Click the Setting ▾ and choose the desired bit rate.

● Select this check box if you want iTunes to play the songs on the CD as you import them.

● Select this check box if you want iTunes to automatically retrieve the names of the CD tracks from the Internet.

● Select this check box if you want the track number to be included with the filenames.

● Select this check box if you want iTunes to employ the Error Correction feature while reading CDs that you insert.

⑦ Click OK.

Did You Know?

You can change what iTunes does by default when you insert a CD into your computer's CD drive. For example, you might want the program to automatically begin playing the CD, or to ask you whether you want to import the CD. To do so, click the On CD Insert ▾ in the Importing tab shown in Steps 5 to 7, and choose the desired option.

Listen to Music Files in iTunes

One of the primary uses of iTunes is as a music player, and so listening to your song files in iTunes is easy. In fact, all that you need to do is click the song you want to hear and click the Play button in the upper-left corner of the iTunes window.

You do have a few more options when it comes to playing music files. For example, you can opt to *shuffle* files — that is, play

them in a random order. You can also repeat playback of a file.

As you become more familiar with iTunes, you may want to create and play your own *playlists*, which are compilations of songs. You can learn more about playlists in Chapter 5.

---

① Click Music in the Source list.

② Click the song you want to hear in the File list.

③ Click the Play button.

● iTunes plays the song.

● The Play button changes to a Pause button.

● A speaker icon (🔊) appears next to the song being played.

Suppose you have borrowed a CD from the library and you want to listen to it to determine whether to purchase it, but you do not want to import the songs into iTunes. Fortunately, iTunes makes it easy to play a CD, either in its entirety or just a few songs.

If iTunes is not already the default player for audio files, you can change the program's settings to make it so. The default player is the program that automatically launches when you insert a CD into your computer's CD drive or attempt to play a music file stored on your hard drive.

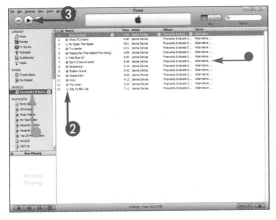

① With iTunes open, insert the CD you want to play in your computer's CD drive.

● The name of the CD displays in the Source list.

● The contents of the CD display in the File list.

② Click the check box next to any song you do not want to hear (☑ changes to ☐).

③ Click the Play button.

iTunes plays the first selected song on the CD.

TIP

Attention!
If your computer is a PC, you can set iTunes as the default player by opening the Edit menu, choosing Preferences, clicking the Advanced tab, clicking the General tab in the Advanced tab, and clicking the Use iTunes as the Default Player for Audio Files check box to select it. On a Mac, click the iTunes menu, choose Preferences, click General, and choose the desired option from the On CD Insert list.

One way to adjust volume in iTunes is to drag the volume slider in the top-left area of the window. To fine-tune iTunes' sound, you can use its Equalizer.

The values across the bottom of the Equalizer window reflect the spectrum of sound frequencies that are audible to humans. The values on the left represent bass frequencies, and the values on the right represent treble frequencies. You adjust the degree to which a frequency is

audible by dragging its corresponding slider, or *fader*. To adjust all frequencies equally, you can drag the Preamp fader upward or downward. For example, you might do this for a song that was recorded at a level that is too quiet or too loud.

In addition to changing Equalizer settings manually, you can also choose from several pre-defined Equalizer settings, many of which are designed for specific genres.

---

① Click View.

② Click Show Equalizer.

● The Equalizer window opens.

③ Drag any of the faders to adjust frequency settings.

④ To use a pre-defined EQ setup, click the button.

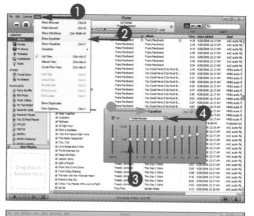

● iTunes displays a list of available EQ pre-sets.

⑤ Click an EQ pre-set.

iTunes applies the selected EQ pre-set.

⑥ Click to close the Equalizer window.

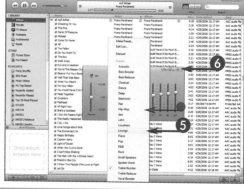

When enabled, the iTunes Visualizer displays colorful "light shows" in the iTunes window, with the effects in the show changing in time with the music.

After you display the Visualizer, you can change how it behaves by pressing certain keys on your computer keyboard. For example, you can tap the Q key to change

how the lines in the free-flowing display change; tap the A key to toggle through various effect options; and tap the Z key to select any of the various available color combinations. When you do this, you can see the name of the currently selected line setting, effect, and color scheme in the upper-right corner of the screen.

① Click View.

② Click Show Visualizer.

iTunes displays the Visualizer.

Note: *To view the Visualizer in full-screen mode (that is, without the iTunes menu bar or other window elements visible), you can click View and choose Full Screen. To return to the regular iTunes window setup, press Esc.*

③ To hide the Visualizer, click View.

④ Click Hide Visualizer.

The iTunes window returns to its normal state.

When you import songs from a CD, iTunes automatically retrieves information about those songs from a Web site called Gracenote. This information includes the name of the songs, the artist, and the name of the album.

If your computer is not connected to the Internet when you import songs, that information is not retrieved. Instead, you simply see a series of generic track names — such as Track 01, Track 02,

Track 03, and so on — with no artist, album, or other information. Fortunately, you can prompt iTunes to obtain this information the next time you connect. If the information returned by Gracenote — also known as CDDB — is not correct, you can edit a track's information from within iTunes. (Be aware that in order for Gracenote to work properly, all tracks from the CD must appear in the list and in their original order.)

① After ensuring that you are connected to the Internet, select the track or tracks for which you want to obtain information.

Note: *To select multiple tracks that are listed together, click the first track in the list and, while holding down the Shift key, click the last track. The first and last tracks, as well as all of the tracks in between, are selected.*

② Click Advanced.

③ Click Get CD Track Names.

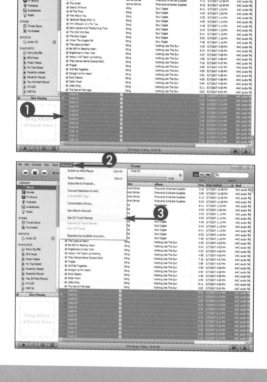

If you selected multiple tracks, iTunes prompts you to confirm that you want to obtain data about them.

④ Click OK.

● iTunes downloads the track information from Gracenote.

More Options

If Gracenote does not contain information about the imported tracks in its database, or if it returns incorrect information, you can edit a track's information from within iTunes. To do so, click the file whose information you want to edit in the File list, click File, and choose Get Info. In the dialog box that appears, click the Info tab and enter the necessary information.

Enter and View Lyrics

Many listeners appreciate it when artists include the lyrics to their music in the liner notes of their CDs. As a result, you might be disappointed that the song files you add to your iTunes library do not include lyrics, whether you are purchasing them from the iTunes Store, importing them from a CD, or downloading them from the Internet.

Fortunately, you can locate the lyrics for many songs online. One way to do so is to simply use your favorite search engine to search for the title of the song whose lyrics you want, along with the word *lyrics*. When you find the lyrics you are looking for, you can then copy and paste them into iTunes.

Keep in mind that the steps in this task are specific to using Internet Explorer 7 and Windows Vista; they may vary depending on your Web browser and operating system.

① Using your Web browser, locate and select the desired lyrics online.

② Select the lyrics you want to copy.

③ Click Page.

④ Click Copy.

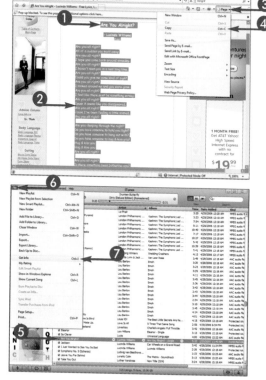

⑤ In iTunes, click to select the song whose lyrics you copied.

⑥ Click File.

⑦ Click Get Info.

98

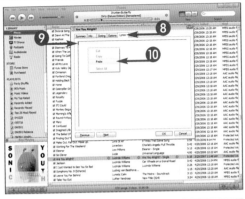

A dialog box opens, containing information about the song.

8 Click the Lyrics tab.

9 Right-click in the tab.

10 Choose Paste.

Note: If you are using a Mac that does not support right-clicking, click in the Lyrics tab, click Edit, and click Paste.

● iTunes pastes the lyrics into the dialog box.

11 Click OK.

Note: To view lyrics you have entered for a song, you can click the song in the File list to select it, click File, choose Get Info, and then click the Lyrics tab.

Did You Know?

Sometimes, albums that are offered for sale in the iTunes Store include interactive booklets. A *booklet* is usually an electronic version of any liner notes or other materials that are meant to accompany the album. For example, a booklet might contain lyrics, photographs of the artist, credits, or similar items. Booklets are marked with a special book graphic (▣).

Fade Songs In and Out

Many albums include gaps of silence between the songs; these gaps may also occur when you listen to your music on iTunes. If you would prefer to listen to the music in your iTunes library without gaps of silence between each song, you can set up iTunes to fade out the song that is currently playing as it fades in the next song in the list. This effect is called *crossfade* (also sometimes referred to as *audio dissolve*). In addition to establishing a crossfade, iTunes enables you to specify how long it takes for songs to fade in and out using a special slider control.

---

① Click Edit (iTunes on a Mac).

② Click Preferences.

An iTunes dialog box opens.

③ Click the Playback tab.

④ Click the Crossfade Playback check box to select it
(☐ changes to ☑).

⑤ Drag the Crossfade Playback slider to the desired time setting.

This setting can be anywhere from 1 second to 12 seconds.

⑥ Click OK.

iTunes applies the crossfade.

Of course, you are not limited to listening to your music library on iTunes. If you have an iPod, you can also listen to your songs while on the go.

You learned in Chapter 3 how to locate a song you want to hear by browsing and searching. Once you locate the desired song, playing it is as simple as pressing the Play button on your iPod.

You do have a few options when it comes to playing music files on your iPod. For example, you can opt to *shuffle* files — that is, play them in a random order. You can also repeat playback of a file. You learned about both of these options in Chapter 3.

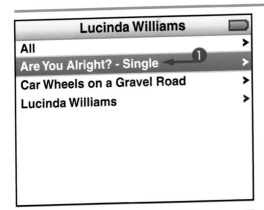

① Either by browsing or searching, locate and select the song file you want to play.

② Press the Play/Pause button on your iPod.

● Your iPod plays the song.

Work with Playlists and Burn CDs with iTunes

An iTunes *playlist* is a compilation of songs (or videos). You might create a playlist for songs you like to listen to as you exercise, songs you want to play at an event, or songs by a particular artist. There is no set limit on the number of playlists you can create. You can also arrange the songs in a playlist however you like, or play them in Shuffle mode.

There are three main types of playlists: standard, which you populate by dragging items from your library to the playlist; a smart playlist, which is generated

automatically by iTunes using rules you establish; and Party Shuffle, which is created automatically by iTunes using randomly selected songs.

After you create a playlist, you can burn the contents of that playlist onto a CD. To do so, you need a computer that houses a CD burner (or an external burner) and a blank CD-RW or CD-R disc (check your burner to determine what type of disc to use). You can burn your files as standard audio CD files, which you can then listen to on nearly any device that plays CDs, or as MP3 files.

Quick Tips

Create a Playlist

Suppose you want to listen to a specific set of songs when you exercise, or that you are planning a dinner party and want to choose the background music. In these cases, you can create an iTunes playlist — that is, a compilation of songs that you select.

There is no set limit on the number of playlists you can create. You can also

specify what songs appear in a playlist, and arrange them in whatever order you like. If you prefer, you can play them back in Shuffle mode.

In addition to creating playlists for music, you can also create them to include audio books, videos, podcasts, Internet radio stations, and other items by following the same basic steps as outlined here.

---

① With Music selected in the Source list, click File.

② Click New Playlist.

● iTunes creates a new, empty playlist.

③ Type a descriptive name for the playlist.

④ In the File list, click a song you want to add to the playlist.

⑤ Drag the selected song to the playlist name in the Source list, and release the mouse button.

iTunes adds the song to the playlist.

⑥ Repeat Steps 4 and 5 to add more songs to the playlist.

Note: *To save time, iTunes allows you to select multiple songs at once and then drag the selected songs to the playlist as a group. Shift-click to select songs listed contiguously in the File list, or Ctrl-click (⌘-click on a Mac) to select songs scattered throughout the File list.*

⑦ To display the contents of a playlist, click it in the Source list.

The contents of the playlist appear in the File list.

Did You Know?

Another way to create a playlist is to first select the songs you want it to contain; then click File and choose New Playlist from Selection. iTunes creates the playlist; if you want, type a new name for the playlist.

After you have populated your playlist, you can edit it. For example, you can add songs by dragging them from your library to the playlist, or remove songs by dragging them from the playlist to the Trash/Recycle bin.

You can also change the order of your playlist. One way is to click the Shuffle button, located in the bottom-left corner of the iTunes window. Another way is to

sort the songs in the list by a category such as name, artist, or album, by clicking the corresponding column header. A third way is by dragging songs to different positions in the playlist, with the left-most column header selected.

You can organize your playlists by placing them in folders. For example, you might create one folder for mellow playlists, and another for upbeat playlists.

MOVE A SONG

1. In the File list, click the left-most column header (marked with a ▼).

2. Click the song you want to move.

3. Drag the song to the desired position in the playlist.

● A line appears in the File list to indicate where iTunes will place the song.

4. Release the mouse button.

● iTunes moves the song.

Note: If iTunes does not move the song, make sure that the iTunes Shuffle function is disabled.

REMOVE A SONG

① Click the song you want to remove.

② Press Delete.

● iTunes removes the song from the playlist.

Note: *Although the song is removed from the playlist, it is not deleted from your library. If you want to permanently remove an item from both the playlist and your library, click the item and press Shift+Delete (⌘+Opt+Del on a Mac).*

TIP

Did You Know?

If you want to determine whether a particular song is in any of your playlists, you may be able to right-click the song and choose Show in Playlist to view a submenu that lists the playlists that contain the selected song. Choose any playlist displayed to open it, with the song selected.

Create a Smart Playlist

In addition to creating standard playlists, you can set up iTunes to generate *smart playlists* — that is, playlists that iTunes populates automatically, using criteria you specify. For example, you might set up a smart playlist to include only those songs

that contain a certain rating, are categorized in a particular genre, or are performed by a given artist. Any songs in your library that match these criteria are added to the smart playlist.

① Click File.

② Click New Smart Playlist.

③ Select the Match the Following Rule check box.

④ Click here and select the first criterion.

⑤ Click here and select the second criterion.

⑥ Type the desired text in this field.

● To add a second set of criteria, you can click the ⊞ button.

⑦ To limit the playlist's size, select the Limit To check box.

⑧ Type the desired value.

⑨ Click here to specify to what the value should apply.

This example selects Items.

⑩ Click here to specify how iTunes should select songs in order to meet the limit.

⑪ To set iTunes to update the playlist when songs that match your criteria are added to your library, select the Live Updating check box.

⑫ Click OK.

iTunes creates a new smart playlist with songs that match your criteria.

⑬ Type a name for the playlist.

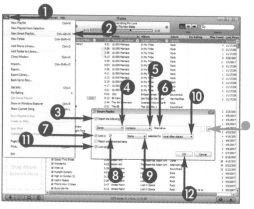

Suppose you create a Smart Playlist that you particularly like. You can convert the Smart Playlist to a standard playlist. Doing so "freezes" the playlist; that is, if you add new songs to iTunes that meet the Smart Playlist's criteria, they will be added to the original Smart Playlist, but not to the standard playlist.

This feature is useful if, for example, you want to create a playlist that contains

many of the same songs as the Smart Playlist; rather than dragging each song from your library individually, you can simply convert a Smart Playlist into a standard playlist and then add and remove songs as needed to perfect it.

In addition to converting a Smart Playlist to a standard playlist, you can also convert a Party Shuffle mix to a standard playlist.

CONVERT A SMART PLAYLIST

① In the source list, click the Smart Playlist you want to convert to a standard playlist.

② Drag the Smart Playlist to the Playlists heading in the source list.

● iTunes creates a standard playlist containing the same content as the Smart Playlist.

③ Type a descriptive name for the new standard playlist.

continued

Convert a Smart Playlist to a Standard Playlist *(continued)*

CONVERT A PARTY SHUFFLE MIX

1 In the source list, click the Party Shuffle entry.

2 Drag the Party Shuffle entry to the Playlists heading in the source list.

● iTunes creates a standard playlist containing the same content as the Party Shuffle.

3 Type a descriptive name for the new standard playlist.

Attention!
In addition to dragging Party Shuffle and Smart Playlist entries to the Playlist heading to convert them to standard playlists, you can also drag the Purchased entry under Store in the source list to the Playlists heading to convert its contents to a standard playlist.

iTunes' Party Shuffle playlist is a special playlist that randomly selects songs from other playlists or from your library. If you like, you can delete songs from Party Shuffle; iTunes simply replaces them with other randomly chosen selections.

You can add songs to Party Shuffle by dragging them onto the playlist, just as you would with a standard playlist. In this way, you can create a playlist that contains

both random content and content you choose.

If you like, you can change the playlists from which Party Shuffle populates itself. When you do this, iTunes removes any randomly chosen tracks that are currently in Party Shuffle. You can also configure Party Shuffle to select songs with higher ratings more often than those with lower ratings.

① Click Party Shuffle in the Source list.

iTunes generates a Party Shuffle playlist.

② Click the Source ⊕ and select the playlist from which you want Party Shuffle to draw songs.

③ Select the Play Higher Rated Songs More Often check box to limit song selections to those with high ratings.

④ Click the Display: x Recently Played Songs ⊕ to indicate how many recently played songs the playlist should include.

⑤ Click the Display: x Upcoming Songs ⊕ to indicate how many upcoming songs the playlist should include.

iTunes updates the playlist to reflect your criteria.

● If you do not like the updated playlist, you can click Refresh to generate a new one using the same criteria.

Publish an iMix or Sport iMix

If you have created a playlist that you want to share with others, you can publish it to the iTunes Store. When you publish a playlist to the iTunes Store, it is called an *iMix* or *Sport iMix*. (Sport iMixes are playlists created with workouts in mind, and are grouped together in the iTunes Store.)

Anyone who visits the iTunes Store can view your iMix, which remains available for one year. Visitors also have the option of rating your iMix.

iMixes can contain as many as 100 songs, and include 30-second previews of each song in the playlist. If someone finds a song on your iMix that they want to buy, they can do so from the page containing your list. (Note that only those songs in your list that are available in the iTunes Store are included in your iMix.) Alternatively, iTunes Store customers can purchase the entire contents of your iMix with the click of a button.

① Click the playlist you want to publish as an iMix or Sport iMix.

② Click File.

③ Click Create an iMix.

An iTunes dialog box appears.

④ Click Create.

Note: *You may be prompted to log in to your iTunes Store account. If so, simply enter the requested information.*

iTunes connects to the iTunes Store.

⑤ Specify whether the playlist should be published as an iMix or a Sport iMix.

⑥ Type a new title for the iMix.

By default, the iMix title matches the title of the original playlist.

⑦ Type a description for the playlist.

⑧ Click Publish.

The iTunes Store informs you that the iMix has been submitted, and that you will be notified by e-mail when it becomes available on the iTunes Store.

⑨ Click Done.

More Options!

To edit and update an iMix or Sport iMix that you have published on the iTunes Store, click the ⊙ to the right of the playlist name in the Source list in the iTunes window. Click the Update button in the dialog box that appears, make the desired changes, and click Publish. You can remove an iMix from the iTunes Store by logging in to your store account, clicking Store, and choosing View My Account.

The iTunes Store enables you to create a wish list — that is, a playlist that stores a list of items you want to purchase at a later date.

When you create a wish list and add a song to it, the song appears in your iTunes File list with a Buy Song button. You can click the Buy Song button to purchase the song. If you like you can publish your wish list as an iMix, enabling others to purchase the music for you.

Even after you purchase a song on your wish list, it remains on the list. However, clicking it results in the playback of the entire song instead of a 30-second preview. In addition, the song's price information is removed.

① With the iTunes Store open on your desktop, click File.

② Click New Playlist.

● iTunes creates a new, empty playlist.

③ Name the playlist Wish List.

④ Locate and click a song on the iTunes Store that you want to add to your wish list.

⑤ Drag the selected song to the wish list in the Source list, and release the mouse button.

iTunes adds the song to the wish list.

⑥ Repeat Steps 4 and 5 to add more songs to the wish list.

⑦ Click Wish List in the Source list.

● iTunes displays the contents of your wish list.

⑧ To purchase a song on the wish list, click Buy Song.

Did You Know?

If a song is not yet available, you might be able to pre-order it. Items that can be pre-ordered feature a Pre-order button; click it to pre-order the item. The iTunes Store e-mails you to notify you when it is available for download. To view or cancel pre-ordered items that are not yet available, click Store, click View My Account, and click Manage Pre-orders.

If you use iTunes to create a playlist, you can burn that playlist to a CD. On average, most CDs can store about 80 minutes of music, which is about 20 songs.

In order to burn a CD, you need a computer that houses a CD burner (or an external burner connected to the computer). You also need a blank CD-RW or CD-R disc (check your burner to determine what type of disc to use).

In addition to burning your music files as standard audio CD files, you can also burn them as MP3 files — this means that you can fit many more songs on a single disc. However, discs containing MP3 files can only be played back on devices that support the MP3 format.

---

① With the playlist you want to burn to CD displayed in iTunes, click Edit.

② Click Preferences.

An iTunes dialog box opens.

③ Click the Advanced tab.

Note: If your playlist contains more songs than can fit on the CD, iTunes prompts you to specify whether you want to burn the playlist onto multiple CDs or cancel the operation.

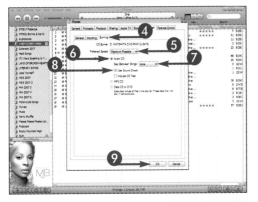

④ Click the Burning tab.

⑤ Click the Preferred Speed ⬆ and choose the desired burn rate.

⑥ Click Audio CD (◎ changes to ◉).

⑦ Click the Gap Between Songs ⬆ and specify how many seconds (if any) should separate each track on the disc.

⑧ Click Use Sound Check if you want all of the songs on the disc to play back at the same volume (☑ changes to ◆).

⑨ Click OK.

⑩ Click Burn Disc.

⑪ Insert a blank disc into your CD drive.

iTunes burns the playlist to disc.

TIP

More Options!

To burn a playlist onto a CD as MP3 files rather than standard CD audio files, click to select the MP3 CD option under Disc Format in the Burning tab. Then click the Burn MP3 CD button in the lower-right corner of the iTunes window and insert a blank CD. Keep in mind that songs in the playlist that are not in MP3 format — for example, songs purchased from the iTunes Store — cannot be burned as MP3 files onto a CD.

Print CD Inserts

When you burn a playlist to CD, you may want to create a CD insert or song list for the disc's jewel case. That way, you can easily keep track of which CDs contain what songs. The insert also lends a certain aesthetic touch to your CD project.

Rather than typing your song list manually, you can use iTunes to generate a pre-designed CD insert. Designs range from simple black-and-white text to inserts featuring a collage of album covers from songs in the playlist. iTunes enables you to preview each design before committing it to print.

---

① Display the playlist for which you want to create an insert in iTunes, and then click File.

② Click Print.

The Print *Playlist Name* dialog box opens.

③ Click CD Jewel Case Insert (○ changes to ◉).

④ Click the Theme ▼ and select a theme from the list that appears.

● A preview of the insert appears with the selected theme.

⑤ When you find a theme you like, click OK.

The Print dialog box opens.

⑥ Click the Number of Copies ◆ to specify how many copies of the insert you want to print.

⑦ Click OK.

iTunes sends the CD insert to your printer.

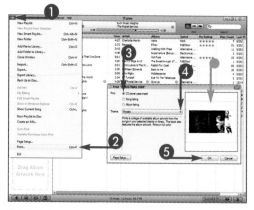

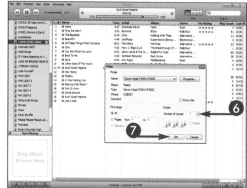

Some iPod models enable you to create a playlist on the go — that is, when the device is not connected to iTunes — by adding songs to its special On-The-Go playlist.

To add items to the On-The-Go playlist, simply display the song, album, artist, or existing playlist on your iPod, and then press and hold down the center button on the device. You can access On-The-Go from the Playlists screen, which is accessible from the Music screen.

After you populate the On-The-Go playlist, you can save it as a separate list, freeing you to create a new On-The-Go playlist.

① Populate the On-The-Go playlist by selecting the desired songs and pressing and holding the Select button on your iPod; then select On-The-Go on the Playlists screen.

To access the Playlists screen, you can select Music in the main iPod screen, and then select Playlists.

The On-The-Go screen appears, listing the songs you have added to the On-The-Go playlist.

② Select Save Playlist.

The saved playlist appears in the Playlists screen.

Enjoy Other Audio Content with iTunes and Your iPod

When you use iTunes and your iPod, you are not limited to enjoying only the music in your iTunes library. Other audio content is also available. For example, if your computer is connected to the Internet, you can use iTunes to listen to Internet radio. You can also subscribe to and download podcasts from the iTunes Store and from other online sources; you can then use iTunes or your iPod to listen to them.

Listening to audio books both on iTunes and your iPod is also an option, whether you purchase them from the iTunes Store or import them from a CD. You can even adjust the speed at which an audio book is read on your iPod, either slowing it down or speeding it up for the listener.

Quick Tips

You can access hundreds of Internet radio stations through iTunes. Station formats include 50s/60s Pop, 70s/80s Pop, Alternative, Ambient, Blues, Classic Rock, Classical, Country, Eclectic, Electronic, Folk, Hip Hop/R&B, International, Jazz, Latino, Pop, Public, Reggae, Religious, Rock, and Talk/Spoken Word.

Unlike music and podcasts that you download from the iTunes Store and save to your computer, Internet radio is *streamed* to your computer. As a result, you cannot stop or pause playback of a station; much like "regular" radio, whatever the station is playing at a given moment is what you hear.

① Click Radio in the Source list.

iTunes displays a list of radio station genres.

② Click the ▶ to the left of the desired radio genre.

iTunes displays a list of stations in the selected format.

③ Double-click a station to listen to it.

Although iTunes does offer direct access to hundreds of Internet radio stations in nearly two dozen genres, there are thousands more Internet radio stations and other types of live streaming feeds — including live-broadcast concerts and sporting events — available online.

Unlike music and podcasts that you download and save to your computer from the iTunes Store and other online

sources, Internet broadcasts are *streamed* to your computer. As a result, you cannot stop or pause playback of an Internet broadcast.

If you know the URL of the Web site that is broadcasting the Internet radio station, concert, sporting event, or other content, and if you are connected to the Internet, you can use iTunes to listen to the stream.

① Click Advanced.

② Click Open Stream.

The Open Stream dialog box opens.

③ Type the URL of the site that hosts the broadcast you want to hear.

An entry appears in your Music File list for the site that is broadcasting the stream.

④ Double-click the entry to listen to the stream.

Download a Podcast Episode from the iTunes Store

A *podcast* — a portmanteau of iPod and broadcast — is a digital media file that is distributed over the Internet.

Unlike Internet radio, which streams content and can only be heard live, a podcast is pre-recorded, downloaded to your computer, and stored there. As a result, you can enjoy the podcast at your leisure, using either iTunes or your iPod.

Typically, a podcast file contains an episode of a radio- or television-style show. You can download individual podcast episodes from the iTunes Store. If you find that you really like a podcast, you can subscribe to it. When you subscribe to a podcast, files for new episodes are downloaded automatically. Whether you download a single episode or subscribe, podcasts are typically free of charge.

① In the main screen of the iTunes Store, click the Podcasts link.

② Locate the page for a podcast you want to hear.

The iTunes Store displays a list of available episodes of the selected podcast.

③ Click Get Episode.

iTunes downloads the podcast episode from the iTunes Store.

Note: *The podcast download may take a few minutes.*

④ To view the progress of the download, click Downloads in the Source list.

● iTunes displays the progress of the download.

⑤ When the download is complete, click Podcasts in the Source list.

● The episode you downloaded appears in the File list.

TIP

More Options!

After you listen to a podcast episode that you downloaded from the iTunes Store, you may want to subscribe to that podcast, in order to receive new episodes of the podcast automatically. You can do so from within iTunes without having to first launch the iTunes Store. To do so, simply click the Subscribe button that appears in the podcast entry in your iTunes Podcast File list.

You can download individual podcast episodes from the iTunes Store. If you find that you really like a podcast, you can subscribe to it. When you subscribe to a podcast, files for new episodes are downloaded automatically.

To subscribe to a podcast that you have downloaded using iTunes, you can click Podcasts in the Source list, and then click the Subscribe button that appears in the podcast's entry in the File list.

If you have not yet downloaded any episodes of the podcast to which you want to subscribe, you can subscribe to the podcast from within iTunes.

You can also unsubscribe from a podcast, thus preventing iTunes from automatically downloading more episodes. To do so, click Podcasts in the Source list, click the podcast from which you want to unsubscribe in the File list, and click the Unsubscribe button at the bottom of the File list.

① In the main screen of the iTunes Store, click the Podcasts link.

② Locate the page for a podcast that you want to hear.

③ Click Subscribe.

An iTunes dialog box appears.

④ Click Subscribe.

iTunes subscribes you to the podcast and downloads the most recent podcast episode from the iTunes Store.

⑤ To view the progress of the download, click Downloads in the Source list.

● iTunes displays the progress of the download.

⑥ When the download is complete, click Podcasts in the Source list.

● The downloaded episode appears in the File list.

Download Podcasts from Other Online Sources

One way to subscribe to a podcast is by using the iTunes Store. But what if the podcast to which you want to subscribe is not available through the iTunes Store? No need to worry. You can still subscribe to and listen to the podcast using iTunes; you just need to know the podcast's Internet address. In most cases, you can determine the podcast's Internet address from its Web page.

To unsubscribe from a podcast, whether you downloaded it from the iTunes Store or from another source, you can click Podcasts in the Source list, click the podcast from which you want to unsubscribe in the File list, and click the Unsubscribe button at the bottom of the File list.

① In the iTunes window, click Advanced.

② Click Subscribe to Podcast.

The Subscribe to Podcast dialog box opens.

③ Type the podcast's Internet address.

④ Click OK.

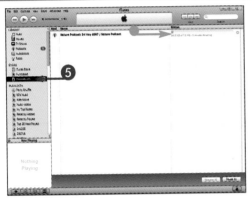

iTunes subscribes you to the podcast and downloads the most recent podcast episode.

⑤ To view the progress of the download, click Downloads in the Source list.

● iTunes displays the progress of the download.

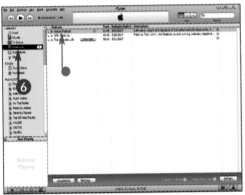

⑥ When the download is complete, click Podcasts in the Source list.

● The episode that was downloaded appears in the File list.

Check It Out!

While the iTunes Store does offer a great selection of podcasts, it only represents a small portion of the podcasts available worldwide. To locate podcasts that are not offered through the iTunes Store, try visiting one of the podcast directories, such as allpodcasts.com, indiepodder.org, or podcastalley.com.

If you subscribe to podcasts using iTunes, you may want to set how frequently iTunes checks for new episodes of your podcasts, whether all available episodes

should be downloaded during the retrieval process, and which and how many episodes should be kept. You can easily establish all these settings in iTunes.

① Click Edit (iTunes on a Mac).

② Click Preferences.

An iTunes dialog box opens.

③ Click the Check for New Episodes ▼ and specify how often iTunes should check for new podcast episodes.

④ Click the When New Episodes Are Available ☑ and specify which episodes iTunes should download.

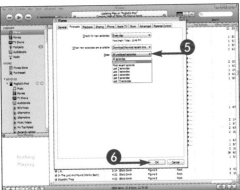

⑤ Click the Keep ☑ and specify which episodes iTunes should keep.

⑥ Click OK.

Attention!

Another way to access podcast settings is to click Podcasts in the source list and, in the screen that appears, click Settings. Doing so opens the dialog box shown in this task.

As mentioned in a previous task, you can subscribe to podcasts, so that iTunes downloads episodes of that podcast automatically. You can specify how many new episodes should be downloaded automatically, how frequently iTunes should check for new episodes, and which episodes are saved by default. To do so, you click Podcasts in the Source list and click the Settings button at the bottom of the File list.

In addition to downloading episodes using the settings you specify, iTunes may also download and display information about episodes that do not meet your criteria — for example, episodes released before you subscribed to the podcast. To download any of these podcast episodes, you can click the Get button in the podcast listing.

① In the Source list, click Podcasts.

iTunes displays a list of podcasts for which you have downloaded episodes.

② Click the ▶ next to a podcast.

iTunes displays a list of available episodes.

- Episodes that have been downloaded are indicated with a check mark ().

- Episodes that are available but that have not been downloaded appear grayed out.

- To download a grayed-out episode, you can click Get.

3️⃣ Double-click the episode you want to hear.

- iTunes plays back the episode.

TIP

Did You Know?

If you encounter any problems with a podcast that you have downloaded from iTunes, click the Report a Concern link below the list of podcasts in your File list. iTunes directs you to a special page on the iTunes Store, enabling you to specify what type of problem you encountered (choices include Offensive Content, Difficulty Playing Episode, and Incorrect Category) and to type additional comments.

Listen to a Podcast on Your iPod

If you sync your iPod with iTunes after downloading a podcast episode, that podcast episode becomes available on your iPod by default. You can then listen to your podcasts while you are on the go.

To access settings that specify which episodes of which podcasts are synced automatically with your iPod, you must first connect your iPod to your computer. Then, in the iTunes Source list, you can click the entry for your iPod under Devices, and click the Podcasts tab in the screen that appears.

① Select Podcasts in the Music screen.

Note: *To access the Music screen, select Music in the main iPod screen.*

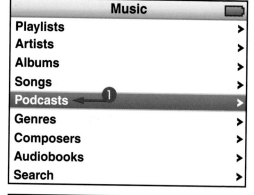

The Podcasts screen appears, displaying a list of podcasts on your iPod.

② Select the podcast you want to hear.

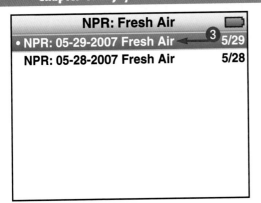

A list of episodes appears for the selected podcast.

③ Select the desired episode.

● Your iPod plays back the podcast.

Did You Know?
If you have disabled syncing, or if your model of iPod does not support the automatic syncing of podcasts, you can add podcasts to your iPod manually. To do so, connect your iPod to your computer. Then click Podcasts in the Source list, click the podcast episode you want to add, and drag it to the entry for your iPod in the Source list (under Devices).

Optimize Settings for Spoken-Word Recordings

By default, iTunes' import settings are geared toward importing music content. If the content you are importing is of the spoken-word variety, such as an audio book, you should adjust iTunes' import settings to optimize the content. Specifically, you set the stereo bit rate, the sample rate, and the channels, as well as apply other voice-optimization settings.

In addition to optimizing iTunes for importing audio books, you can also optimize the program for importing podcasts.

① Click Edit (iTunes on a Mac).

② Click Preferences.

An iTunes dialog box opens.

③ Click the Advanced tab.

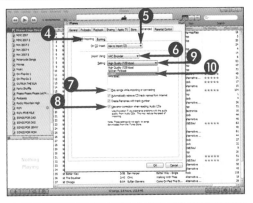

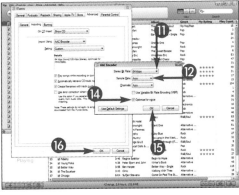

④ Click the Importing tab.

⑤ Click the On CD Insert ▪ and choose Show CD.

⑥ Click the Import Using ▪ and choose AAC Encoder.

⑦ Click the Play Songs While Importing or Converting check box to deselect it (☑ changes to ☐).

⑧ Click the Use Error Correction When Reading Audio CDs check box to select it (☐ changes to ☑).

⑨ Click the Setting ▪.

⑩ Click Custom.

The AAC Encoder dialog box opens.

⑪ Click the Stereo Bit Rate ▪ and choose 64 kbps.

⑫ Click the Sample Rate ▪ and choose Auto.

⑬ Click the Channels ▪ and choose Auto.

⑭ Click the Optimize for Voice check box to select it (☐ changes to ☑).

⑮ Click OK to close the AAC Encoder dialog box.

⑯ Click OK to close the iTunes dialog box.

iTunes applies the settings you selected.

Import an Audio Book from CD

If you have purchased an audio book on CD or borrowed one from your library that you want to make available on iTunes and your iPod, you can import it.

However, before you do this, you must optimize your import settings for the

spoken word. Follow the steps in the previous task, "Optimize Settings for Spoken-Word Recordings," and then proceed with the following steps to import your audio book.

---

① Insert the first CD from the audio book that you want to import.

A list of tracks on the CD appears in the iTunes File list.

② Press Ctrl+A (⌘+A on a Mac) on your keyboard to select all of the tracks on the CD.

③ Click Advanced.

④ Click Join CD Tracks.

● The tracks on the CD are merged into a single track.

⑤ Click Import CD.

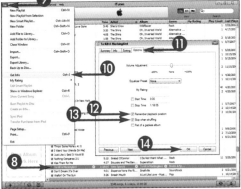

- iTunes imports the CD.

⑥ When the import operation is complete, eject the CD.

⑦ Click Music in the Source list.

Note: Audio books that you import in this manner do not appear under Audiobooks in the iTunes Source list or the iPod menu structure. Instead, they appear as files in your music library. To make an audio book's files easier to find, consider creating a special playlist for them.

⑧ Locate and select the file that you just imported.

⑨ Click File.

⑩ Click Get Info.

⑪ In the Get Info dialog box that opens, click the Options tab.

⑫ Select the Remember Playback Position check box.

⑬ Select the Skip When Shuffling check box.

⑭ Click OK.

⑮ Repeat Steps 1 to 14 for each of the audio book's remaining CDs.

TIP

Caution!

Before you begin, if you have borrowed the audio book from your local library, you should delete the audio book after listening to it. You should also not share the copied version with others. Failure to adhere to these rules is a violation of the audio book's copyright.

If you are a dedicated bibliophile, you can use iTunes and your iPod to listen to audio books, tens of thousands of which are available for purchase at the iTunes Store. Available titles, which start at just a few dollars, include blockbuster novels, best-selling nonfiction, self-help, and language instruction.

After you purchase and download an audio book from the iTunes Store, it becomes available in your iTunes

Audiobooks library. To access the library, you can click Audiobooks in the Source list.

If you need to take a break while listening to an audio book on iTunes, you can easily find your place in the story when you return to it. Both iTunes and your iPod keep track of where you left off. If your iPod and iTunes are synced, you can even pick up on one where you left off on the other.

---

① In the Source list, click Audiobooks.

Note: If the audio book you want to listen to was imported from a CD, it does not appear under Audiobooks in the iTunes Source list. Instead, it appears as a group of files in your music library.

A list of audio books that you have downloaded from the iTunes Store appears.

② Click the audio book file that you want to hear.

③ Click Play.

● iTunes plays back the audio book.

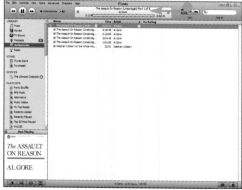

④ Click Chapters.

Note: *The Chapters menu appears only if your audio book includes chapter markers.*

⑤ Click the chapter that you want to go to.

● iTunes begins playing back the audio book at the chapter you chose.

Did You Know?

To enable you to switch to a different chapter while listening to an audio book, iTunes offers a special Chapters menu, which displays only when you have selected Audiobooks in the Source list and clicked an audio book file that contains chapter markers. Simply click the Chapters menu to open it and choose the desired chapter from the File list that appears.

If you sync your iPod with iTunes after downloading an audio book, that audio book becomes available on your iPod by default. You can then listen to your audio books while you are on the go.

If you need to take a break from the audio book you are listening to with your iPod, you can find your place in the story when you return to it. Both iTunes and your iPod keep track of where you left off. If your iPod and iTunes are synced, you can even pick up on one where you left off on the other.

① Select Music in the main iPod screen.

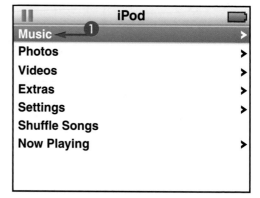

The Music screen appears.

② Select Audiobooks.

Note: If the audio book that you want to listen to was imported from a CD, it does not appear under Audiobooks in the iPod menu structure. Instead, it appears in the Music folder.

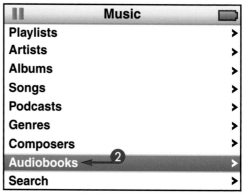

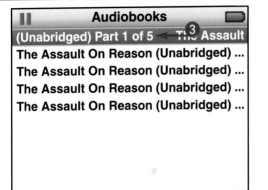

The Audiobooks screen appears, displaying a list of audio books on your iPod.

3 Select the audio book that you want to hear.

● Your iPod plays back the audio book.

Did You Know?

In addition to adjusting audio settings such as volume and EQ, you can also set a speed option that applies to audio books. That is, you can specify whether the text in the audio book is read at a normal speed, slower, or faster. To change the speed setting, choose Settings in the main iPod screen, choose Audiobooks, and choose Slower, Normal, or Faster.

Chapter

7

Enjoy Video with iTunes and Your iPod

Although iTunes and the iPod were originally developed as audio players, Apple expanded the purview of both to include video in 2005.

One way to obtain video for use with iTunes and the iPod is by purchasing it from the iTunes Store. There you can find episodes of television shows, music videos, short films, and feature-length movies, all available for download. In addition, movie trailers and video podcasts can be downloaded from the iTunes Store free of charge. You can download video content just as you do any other type of content from the iTunes Store; for more information, refer to the task, "Purchase Content from the iTunes Store," in Chapter 2.

You can also download videos from other online sources, such as Google Video. After you download a video to your computer, you can import it into iTunes.

In order to play videos using iTunes, your computer must have adequate processing power. As of this writing, you require a Windows PC with at least a 2.0 GHz processor, 512MB of RAM and at least 32MB VRAM, and Windows 2000 or later; if you are a Mac user, you require a 1GHz G4 or better system with Mac OS X 10.3.9 or later, with 16MB of VRAM. In addition, QuickTime 7.1.3 (Windows) or 7.1.5 (Mac) or later must be installed.

Quick Tips

Purchase Multiple Episodes of a TV Show at the iTunes Store

As of this writing, the iTunes Store offers episodes of more than 350 television shows for purchase.

Purchasing a single episode of a television show from the iTunes Store is just like purchasing any other type of content: You locate the episode you want to purchase and click the Buy button.

The iTunes Store offers three other options for purchasing episodes of television shows: Season Pass, Multi-Pass,

and Buy Season. A *Season Pass* enables you to purchase an entire season of a program; in contrast, a *Multi-Pass* allows you to buy a set number of episodes. iTunes notifies you through e-mail as new episodes are posted (usually within a few days of being aired on television) and places the new episode in your download queue. The third option, *Buy Season*, enables you to purchase all of the episodes of a season that has aired in its entirety.

① In the iTunes Store, click TV Shows.

② Locate the show for which you want to purchase episodes.

③ Click Buy Season Pass, Buy Multi-Pass, or Buy Season.

This example selects the Buy Season option.

④ When prompted, click Buy.

iTunes begins the download process.

⑤ Click Downloads in the Source list.

● iTunes displays the progress of the download operation.

⑥ When the download process is complete, click TV Shows in the Source list.

● iTunes displays a list of available episodes.

Did You Know?

To view television shows that you have purchased from iTunes, click TV Shows in the Source list. A list of available shows appears; simply double-click the show you want to watch. By default, iTunes plays back the show in the artwork viewer, located below the Source list. To find out how to play back the show in a larger format, see the task, "Watch a Video in iTunes."

Import a Video from Your Computer to iTunes

In addition to downloading video content from the iTunes Store, you can also download videos from other sources, such as Internet sites, to your computer's hard drive.

Once a video file is downloaded to your computer, you can import that video file into iTunes. You can then use iTunes to play back the video.

If you like, you can view information about a video, regardless of whether it has been downloaded from the iTunes Store or imported from your computer. This information includes the file type, file size, bit rate, and sample rate of the video.

---

1 Click File.

2 Click Import.

The Import dialog box opens.

3 Locate and select the video you want to import.

4 Click Open.

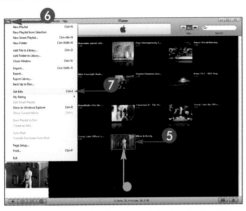

● iTunes imports the video.

⑤ To view information about the imported video, click the video in the File list.

⑥ Click File.

⑦ Click Get Info.

A dialog box appears, displaying information about the selected video, such as the file size and length.

TIP

Important!

In order to import and play back a video using iTunes, that video must be QuickTime compatible (that is, the filename must end in .mov or .mp4). If the video you want to import is not QuickTime compatible, you may need to use some type of third-party software, such as QuickTime Pro, to convert it. For more information, visit www.apple.com/quicktime/pro/win.html.

You can use iTunes to watch any videos that you purchase from the iTunes Store or that you import from your computer. By default, iTunes displays videos in the artwork viewer, located below the Source list. (If the artwork viewer is not displayed, click View and choose Show Artwork.)

You control playback of the video by using the controls in the upper-left corner of the iTunes window.

If you would like to view your video in a larger format, you can easily do so by playing back the video and choosing a different size option from the View menu.

① Click Movies in the iTunes Source list.

Note: If the video you want to watch is a television episode, click TV Shows in the Source list. If it is a video podcast, click Podcasts.

② Double-click the video you want to watch.

● iTunes plays back the video in the artwork viewer.

③ To change the playback format, click View.

④ Click the desired view option.

This example chooses the Full Screen option.

iTunes plays back the video in full-screen mode.

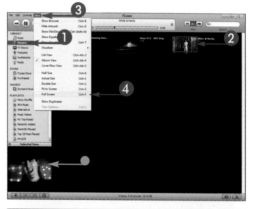

If you have a video iPod, you can use it to watch your videos. However, you may first need to optimize the video for playback in your iPod, especially if the video was imported into iTunes. Be aware that the optimization process can take several minutes — longer if the file is large and your computer is slow. A copy of the un-optimized version of the video remains in your iTunes library.

After you have optimized a video, you can port it to your iPod just as you would any other type of content: by syncing the iPod with iTunes.

① Click the video that you want to optimize.

② Click Advanced.

③ Click Convert Selection for iPod.

● iTunes optimizes the selected video for playback on your iPod.

You can use iTunes to watch any videos that you purchase from the iTunes Store or that you import from your computer (assuming the imported videos are optimized). You can also use your iPod for the same purpose. To do so, you must sync your iPod with iTunes after downloading or importing (and optimizing) the video.

You can adjust certain video-related settings, such as the brightness and aspect ratio, on your iPod to improve your

viewing experience. To access the Brightness setting, select Settings in the main iPod window, select Brightness from the list that appears, and use the click wheel to choose the desired brightness setting. You can also specify the aspect ratio (that is, whether the video plays back in widescreen or standard format) by selecting Video in the main iPod screen, selecting Video Settings in the Video screen, and selecting Widescreen to toggle that setting on or off.

① Select Videos in the main iPod screen.

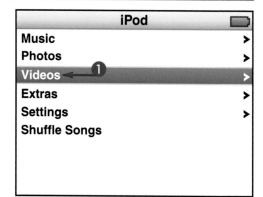

② Select Movies in the Videos screen.

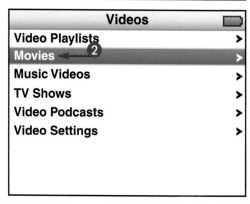

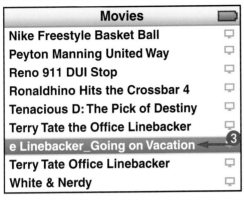

Movies	
Nike Freestyle Basket Ball	💻
Peyton Manning United Way	💻
Reno 911 DUI Stop	💻
Ronaldhino Hits the Crossbar 4	💻
Tenacious D: The Pick of Destiny	💻
Terry Tate the Office Linebacker	💻
e Linebacker_Going on Vacation	❸
Terry Tate Office Linebacker	💻
White & Nerdy	💻

The Movies screen appears, displaying a list of movies on your iPod.

❸ Select the movie you want to watch.

Ron Felcher
C.E.O., Felcher & Sons

● Your iPod plays back the movie.

Attention!
These steps outline how to locate videos that are categorized as movies on your iPod. If the video you want to watch is a music video or an episode of a television show, you can simply select the appropriate option in the Videos screen.

Watch a Video Podcast on Your iPod

If, after downloading a video podcast episode, you sync your iPod with iTunes, that video podcast episode will be available on your iPod by default. You can then view your video podcasts while you are on the go.

To access settings that specify which episodes of which video podcasts are synced automatically with your iPod, first connect your iPod to your computer. Then, in the iTunes source list, click the entry for your iPod under Devices, and click the Podcasts tab in the screen that appears.

---

① Select Video Podcasts in the Video screen.

Note: *To access the Video screen, select Video in the main iPod screen.*

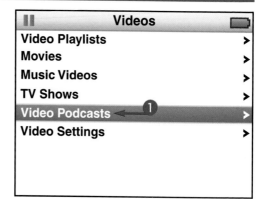

The Video Podcasts screen appears, displaying a list of video podcasts on your iPod.

② Select the video podcast you want to watch.

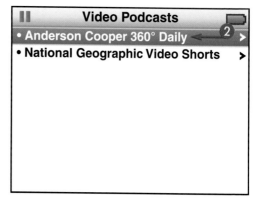

A list of episodes of the selected video podcast appears.

3 Select the desired episode.

● Your iPod plays back the video podcast.

Check It Out!

While the iTunes Store does boast a great selection of video podcasts, its offerings only scratch the surface of the video podcasts available worldwide. To locate video podcasts not offered through the iTunes Store, try visiting videopodcasts.tv, an online directory of video podcasts.

Explore iPod Extras

Most people purchase an iPod for listening to music and viewing video content. However, this doesn't mean that the iPod cannot be put to use in other capacities. For example, you can use your iPod to play games, which you can purchase from the iTunes Store. You can also use your iPod to store photos, and even run a photo slideshow.

You can also use your iPod for more practical purposes. For example, you can

use the iPod Clock as an alarm clock and to track multiple time zones. Indeed, your iPod can operate as a personal digital assistant (PDA). You can sync your iPod with Microsoft Outlook or iCal and Address Book to store your contacts and calendar entries. You can also use your iPod to store notes to yourself and, with the use of special recording hardware, you can record and store voice memos. A stopwatch feature is also included.

Quick Tips

Video iPods include a few pre-installed games by default. These include Brick, which is similar to the classic video game Breakout; Music Quiz, which tests your knowledge of the songs on your iPod; Parachute, a traditional shoot-'em-up; and, of course, Solitaire. You use the click wheel and buttons on your iPod to control game play.

In addition to playing these pre-installed games, you can also use your iPod to play games that you purchase from the iTunes Store. These games include Pac-Man, Ms. Pac-Man, Texas Hold 'Em, and Sudoku.

① In the main iPod screen, select Extras.

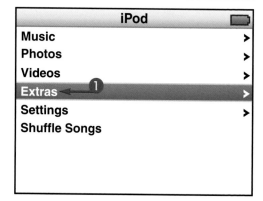

The Extras screen appears.

② Select Games.

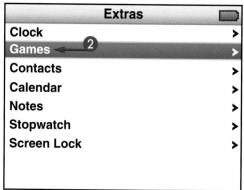

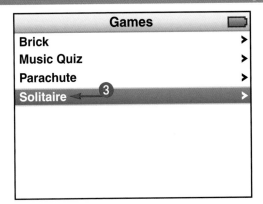

The Games screen appears.

③ Select the game you want to play.

This example selects Solitaire.

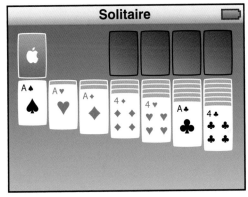

Your iPod launches the game that you selected.

More Options!

As mentioned, you can purchase additional games for your iPod from the iTunes Store. To do so, click the iPod Games link in the left side of the iTunes Store window, locate the desired game, and click Buy Game. After iTunes downloads the game, sync iTunes with your iPod. Note that you cannot play games in iTunes; they can only be played on your iPod.

Load and View Photos on Your iPod

If you store digital photographs on your computer, you can load those photographs onto your iPod. You can choose whether all photos are loaded, or only the photos in a particular folder on your computer's hard drive.

After you load your digital photos onto your iPod, they display in contact-sheet form — that is, they display in a small thumbnail format. To view a specific photo in a larger format, you can simply use your click wheel to scroll through the thumbnail images until the desired photo is highlighted. You can then click the Select button in the center of the click wheel.

---

① Connect your iPod to your computer.

② Click the entry for your iPod in the iTunes Source list.

③ Click the Photos tab.

④ Select the Sync Photos From check box.

⑤ Click the Sync Photos From ⬍ and select the folder on your hard drive that contains the photos that you want to load on your iPod.

● To load all photos in the selected folder onto your iPod, you can click All Photos.

● To load only photos that are stored in certain subfolders, you can click Selected Folders.

● If you choose to include photos in selected folders only, you can click the check box next to each applicable folder.

⑥ Click Apply.

⑦ When iTunes finishes syncing with your iPod, click the ⏏ next to the entry for your iPod in the Source list to eject it.

⑧ On the main iPod screen, click Photos.

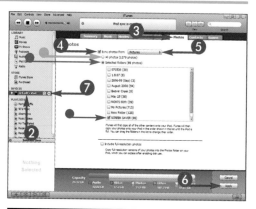

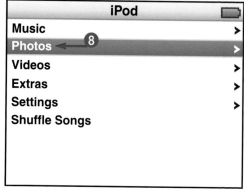

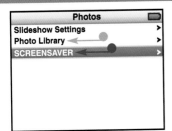

The Photos screen opens.

● You can click Photo Library to view all photos that are stored on your iPod.

● To view only the photos in a particular folder, you can select the folder name.

Thumbnail versions of your photos appear on the iPod screen.

⑨ Select a photo that you want to see.

The photo displays on the iPod's screen.

More Options!
Macs come with the iLife suite, whose applications can often utilize each other's data. This means that iTunes can work with photos stored in iPhoto, and Mac users can sync their iPods with their iPhoto albums.

In addition to storing your digital photos on your iPod, you can also use it to generate a slideshow of those photos. However, you must first establish the settings for slideshows. For example, your iPod enables you to choose how long each image displays, whether images should be repeated or shuffled, and what type of transition effect, if any, should be used when switching from one image to the next. You can also choose to play back the songs in a particular playlist during the slideshow.

After you have established your slideshow settings, you can run the slideshow by selecting the desired folder in the iPod Photos screen and then pressing Play. To pause and restart the slideshow, you press the Play/Pause button on your iPod; you can skip forward or backward by pressing the Next/Fast-Forward or Previous/Rewind button.

① On the main iPod screen, select Photos.

The Photos screen appears.

② Select Slideshow Settings.

The Slideshow Settings screen appears.

③ Select Time Per Slide.

The Next Slide screen appears.

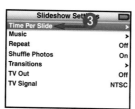

④ Select the desired display duration.

Note: If you select Manual, you can move from one slide to the next by pressing the Next/Fast-Forward button.

⑤ Press the Menu button to return to the Slideshow Settings screen.

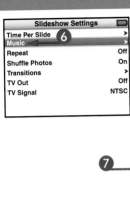

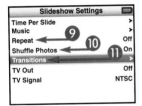

⑥ Select Music.

The Slideshow Music screen appears, listing the playlists on your iPod.

⑦ Select the playlist you want to use as background music for your slideshow.

⑧ Press the Menu button to return to the Slideshow Settings screen.

⑨ Toggle the Repeat option off or on, depending on whether you want the slideshow to repeat.

⑩ Toggle the Shuffle Photos option off or on, depending on whether you want photos to appear in order or at random.

⑪ Select Transitions.

The Transitions screen appears.

⑫ Select the desired transition effect. Your iPod displays this effect when moving from one photo in your slideshow to the next.

Did You Know?

You can use an iPod AV cable to connect your iPod to the RCA inputs on your television to play back your slideshow. Follow the directions that came with the cable to hook up the device. Then toggle the television Out option in your iPod's Slideshow Settings screen to On. If you do not get a signal after you connect your iPod to your television, try toggling the TV Signal setting from NTSC to PAL.

If you like, you can use your iPod as a timepiece. If you use Mac OS X, your iPod's clock syncs with your computer's clock automatically. If not, you can set the time from within your iPod by selecting your geographic region and indicating whether daylight savings should apply.

You are not limited to using a single clock on your iPod. For example, if you frequently conduct business with people on the other side of the globe, you can set up a second clock for that geographic region. Alternatively, you might set up a second clock while you are on a vacation to keep track of local time; upon your return, you can delete the additional clock. To delete a clock, you can select the clock in the Clock screen, choose Delete This Clock, and select Delete.

① Select Extras in the main iPod screen.

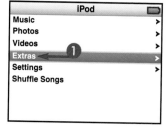

The Extras screen opens.

② Select Clock.

The Clock screen opens.

③ Select the existing clock to set the correct time.

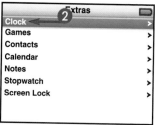

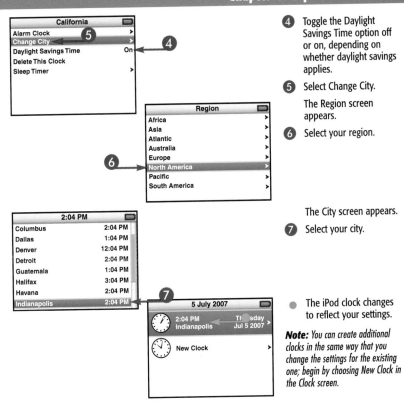

④ Toggle the Daylight Savings Time option off or on, depending on whether daylight savings applies.

⑤ Select Change City.

The Region screen appears.

⑥ Select your region.

The City screen appears.

⑦ Select your city.

● The iPod clock changes to reflect your settings.

Note: *You can create additional clocks in the same way that you change the settings for the existing one; begin by choosing New Clock in the Clock screen.*

More Options!

To change the date (and time) setting, select Settings in the main iPod screen and choose Date & Time. In the Date & Time screen, choose Set Date & Time; then use your click wheel to change the hour, minute, AM/PM, day, month, and year settings, pressing the Next/Fast-Forward button to move from field to field. You can also change the time zone and other date and time settings from the Date & Time screen.

Set an Alarm

You can set up your iPod to sound an alarm at the time you specify. The sound can be a beep, or your iPod can begin playing a song in one of your playlists at the proper time.

Note that if you choose the beep sound, your iPod emits the sound from its internal speaker. As a result, it will be audible even if your iPod is not connected to speakers. However, if you choose a song as your alarm sound, you need to connect your iPod to speakers or wear your headphones in order to hear the sound.

In addition to setting an alarm, you can also use your iPod's Sleep Timer function to automatically switch off your iPod after a period of time that you specify.

---

① Select Extras in the main iPod screen.

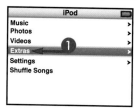

The Extras screen opens.

② Select Clock.

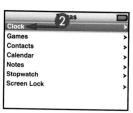

The Clock screen opens.

③ Select the clock for which you want to set an alarm.

④ Select Alarm Clock.

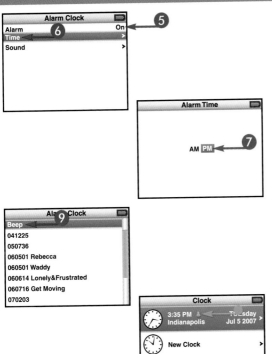

The Alarm Clock screen appears.

5 Toggle the Alarm option on.

6 Select Time.

7 Use your click wheel to change the hour, minute, and AM/PM settings, by pressing the Next/Fast-Forward button to move from field to field, and again to return to the Alarm Clock screen.

8 Select Sound in the Alarm Clock screen.

9 Select the sound that you want to use with the alarm.

10 Press the Menu button three times to return to the main Clock screen.

● A (( )) icon indicates that an alarm has been set.

More Options!

To set your iPod's sleep timer, select your clock in the main Clock screen, choose Sleep Timer in the screen that appears, specify how long you want the iPod to wait before switching itself off, and then press the Menu button. A special ⏰ icon appears when you play back content on your iPod, indicating how much longer the iPod plays before shutting itself off.

Use the iPod Stopwatch

Many people use their iPods to listen to music while exercising. To increase the iPod's usefulness, Apple has included a Stopwatch function to help you keep track of your workout's duration. If you are running on a track, you can use your iPod Stopwatch feature to keep track of lap times. You can also use the Stopwatch and listen to music at the same time.

As you work out, the Stopwatch keeps a session log. When you finish your session, you can view this log, which includes the date and time at which the session took place, and the total session time. If applicable, it also includes the shortest lap time, the longest lap time, the average lap time, and a list of each individual lap time.

---

① In the Extras screen, select Stopwatch.

Note: *To view the Extras screen, select Extras in the main iPod screen.*

The Stopwatch screen appears.

② Select Timer.

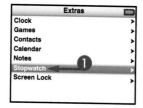

③ To start the timer, select Start.

④ If your workout involves completing laps, track each lap by first using your click wheel to highlight the Lap button. Then, as you complete a lap, press the Select button on your iPod to record the lap time.

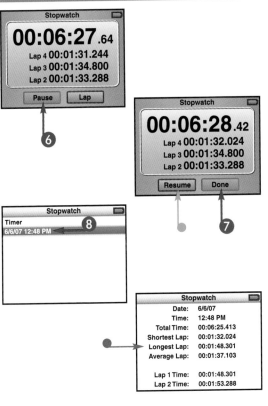

⑤ With the Lap button still highlighted, press the Select button on your iPod each time you complete a lap.

⑥ As you near the finish, use your click wheel to highlight the Pause button; then, when you finish your workout, press the Select button on your iPod to pause the timer.

● If you want to resume your workout, you can select Resume.

⑦ When you finish your workout, use your click wheel to highlight the Done button and press the Select button on your iPod.

⑧ To view a summary of your workout session, select the session in the Stopwatch screen.

● The session log appears, summarizing your workout.

Remove It!

Your iPod can store as many as five session logs, which you can view at any time. As soon as you begin logging a sixth session, the oldest log is deleted to make room. To delete a different log, select it in the Stopwatch screen. When the details of the session display, press the Select button on your iPod and select Delete in the screen that appears.

In addition to using your iPod for entertainment purposes, you can also use it as a personal digital assistant (PDA). For example, you can set up your iPod to store your contacts so that you can access them while you are on the go. In order to do so, you must use Microsoft Outlook 2003 or later, Microsoft Outlook Express, or Windows Contacts as your contact-management program on your computer.

You transfer your contacts to your iPod through a sync operation. Any new contacts that you add to your contact-management program are ported to your iPod the next time you sync. Once your contacts have been transferred to your iPod, you can access them from the Extras screen.

① Connect your iPod to your computer.

② Click the entry for your iPod in the iTunes Source list.

③ Click the Contacts tab.

④ Select the Sync Contacts From check box.

⑤ Click the Sync Contacts From ⬍ and select the program that you use to manage contacts on your computer.

● If you want digital images that you have associated with your contacts to appear on your iPod, you can select Include Contacts' Photos.

⑥ Click Apply.

⑦ When iTunes finishes syncing with your iPod, click the ⏏ next to the entry for your iPod in the Source list to eject it.

⑧ On the main iPod screen, select Extras.

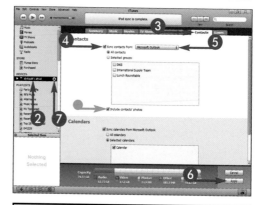

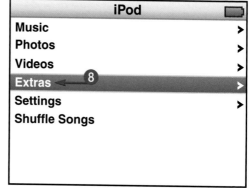

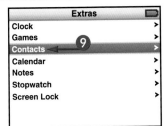

The Extras screen
appears.

9 Select Contacts.

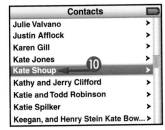

The Contacts screen
appears.

10 Select the contact whose
information you want to
view.

● The contact's
information appears on
the iPod screen.

Did You Know?

Another way to transfer contacts onto your iPod is to first enable your iPod
as a hard drive. Then connect your iPod to your computer and copy your
contacts (or other items) to it just as you would to any other external hard
drive. For more information, see the task, "Use Your iPod as a Storage
Drive," later in this chapter.

Change Contact Settings

You can opt to use your iPod to store your contacts so you can access them while on the go. (Note that in order to do so, you must use Microsoft Outlook 2003 or later, Microsoft Outlook Express, Windows Contacts, or Apple iCal as your contacts-management program on your computer.)

You transfer your contacts to your iPod via a sync operation. After you do, you can access them from the Extras screen. If you like, you can change how your contacts are displayed – for example, opting to sort them by last name instead of by first name.

① In the main iPod screen, select Settings.

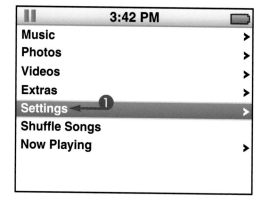

The Settings screen appears.

② Select Contacts.

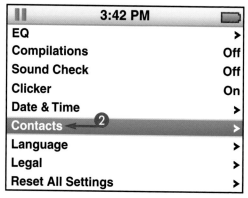

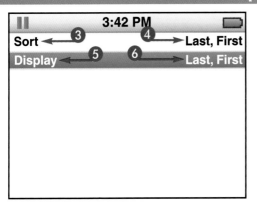

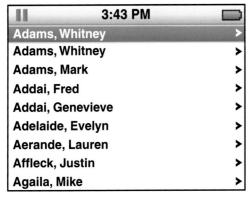

The Contacts screen appears.

③ Using the click wheel, highlight the Sort entry.

④ Press the Select button on the iPod to toggle between Last, First and First, Last.

⑤ Using the click wheel, highlight the Display entry.

⑥ Press the Select button on the iPod to toggle between Last, First and First, Last.

iTunes again displays your library in its entirety.

Attention!
If, after adjusting your iPod's settings, you decide you preferred the device's original configuration, you can revert to it. To do so, select Settings in the main iPod screen, select Reset All Settings in the Settings screen, and select Reset in the Reset All screen that appears.

If you use Microsoft Outlook 2003 or later, Microsoft Outlook Express, or Windows Calendar to maintain your calendar on your computer, you can port your calendar entries to your iPod.

You transfer your calendar entries to your iPod through a sync operation. Any new calendar entries that you add to your calendar program are ported to your iPod the next time you sync. Once your calendar entries have been transferred to your iPod, you can access them from the Extras screen.

If you like, you can configure your iPod to emit an alarm as calendar events draw nearer to the time interval that you chose.

① Connect your iPod to your computer.

② Click the entry for your iPod in the iTunes Source list.

③ Click the Contacts tab.

④ Select the Sync Calendars From check box.

You may need to scroll down a bit to see this option.

● To load all calendars that you maintain onto your iPod, you can click All Calendars.

● To load only selected calendars, you can click Selected Calendars.

● If you chose to include selected calendars only, you can click the check box next to each applicable calendar.

⑤ Click Apply.

⑥ When iTunes finishes syncing with your iPod, click the ⏏ next to the entry for your iPod in the Source list to eject it.

⑦ In the main iPod screen, select Extras.

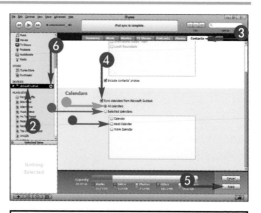

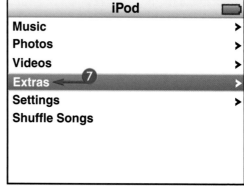

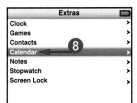

The Extras screen appears.

⑧ Select Calendar.

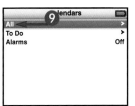

The Calendars screen appears.

⑨ If you have synced multiple calendars to your iPod, select All.

Note: *If you want your iPod to sound or display an alarm to notify you of upcoming events, toggle the Alarms setting; the options are Beep, Silent, and Off.*

⑩ Select a date for which you want to view calendar events.

● Events occurring on the selected day are displayed.

Did You Know?

When you sync your calendar with your iPod, your tasks list is also synced. To view upcoming tasks on your iPod, select Extras in the main iPod screen, select Calendar in the Extras screen, and select To Do in the Calendars screen.

In addition to storing and playing music, video, and games, your iPod also functions as a read-only personal digital assistant (PDA). For example, your iPod can store all or some of the contacts in your Mac's Address Book.

iTunes syncs your Mac's Address Book to your iPod as directed on the Contacts tab when your iPod is connected and selected

in the iTunes source list. Each time you sync your iPod (either automatically or via the Apply button), new entries in your Address Book are moved to the iPod and old entries on your iPod that have been removed from Address Book are deleted. Once your contacts are on your iPod, you can access them via the iPod's Extras screen.

① Connect your iPod to your computer.

② Click the entry for your iPod in the iTunes Source list.

③ Click the Contacts tab.

④ Select the Sync Address Book contacts check box.

● To load all contacts onto your iPod, you can click All contacts.

● To load only selected groups of contacts, you can click Selected groups.

● If you chose to sync only the contacts in selected groups, click the check box next to each desired group.

Note: If a contact's Address Book card includes a photo, that photo will also be available on your iPod.

⑤ Click Apply.

⑥ When iTunes finishes syncing with your iPod, click the ⏏ next to your iPod's entry in the Source list to eject it.

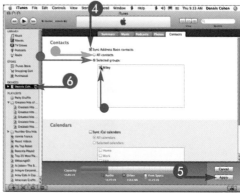

If you use iCal to maintain your calendars on your Mac, you can synchronize your calendars to your iPod.

Any new calendars or calendar entries that you create in iCal are ported to your iPod the next time you sync. The calendar

entries on your iPod are accessible from the Extras screen.

If you like, you can configure your iPod to emit an alarm as calendar events draw nearer to the time interval that you chose.

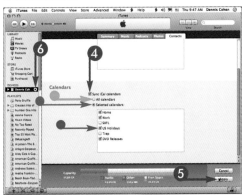

1 Connect your iPod to your computer.

2 Click the entry for your iPod in the iTunes Source list.

3 Click the Contacts tab.

4 Select the Sync iCal Calendars check box.

You may need to scroll down a bit to see this option depending upon your iTunes window size, your Mac's screen size, and the screen resolution at which you're operating.

● To sync all your iCal calendars onto your iPod, click All Calendars.

● To load only selected calendars, click Selected calendars.

● If you chose to sync only selected calendars, click the check box next to each desired calendar.

5 Click Apply.

6 When iTunes finishes syncing with your iPod, click the ⏏ next to your iPod's entry in the Source list to eject it.

Use Your iPod as a Storage Device

Although you can use your iPod to listen to music and watch videos, did you know that you can also use it as a storage device for data files? This might come in handy if, for example, you need to transfer a file from one computer to another.

To use your iPod as a storage device, you must enable it for disk use. You access this setting by connecting your iPod to your computer and viewing the Summary screen that appears in iTunes.

When your iPod is enabled for disk use, an icon for the device appears on the desktop (Mac), or in the Windows folder structure as the next available drive letter, whenever it is connected to a computer.

① Connect your iPod to your computer.

② Click the entry for your iPod in the iTunes Source list.

③ In the Summary tab, select the Enable Disk Use check box.

④ Click Apply.

The iPod is enabled for disk use.

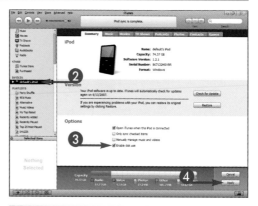

● Your computer now recognizes the iPod as a storage device. In this case, because the iPod is connected to a Windows computer, it is assigned the next available drive letter. If it were connected to a Mac, an icon for the iPod would appear on the desktop and in Finder window sidebars.

⑤ Double-click the icon representing the iPod.

- The iPod's folder structure is revealed.

6 Locate and select a file that you want to store on your iPod.

7 Drag the selected file to the window containing the iPod's folder structure.

- The file is saved on your iPod.

Note: To move a file from your iPod to a computer, simply connect the iPod to the desired computer, reveal its folder structure as described here, and drag the file to the desired location on the computer.

Caution!

If you have enabled your iPod for disk use, you must eject the device properly. To do so, click the ⏏ next to the entry for your iPod in the iTunes Source list. When your iPod no longer appears in the Source list, you can safely disconnect your iPod from your computer. If the computer to which the iPod is connected is not running iTunes, eject it as you would any other hardware device.

If you have enabled your iPod for use as a storage device, you can store files of all types on the iPod. However, in most cases, you cannot actually view these files from within the iPod; the iPod acts only as a conduit.

That said, you can view text files, or Notes, on your iPod. To create a text file, you can use a simple word processor such as TextEdit (Mac) or WordPad (PC). You

can then save the document that you create as a text document by opening the Format menu and choosing Make Plain Text (TextEdit), or by opening the File menu, choosing Save As, and selecting Text Document from the File As Type list (WordPad).

After you create a text file, you can copy it to your iPod, where you can view the file at any time.

---

1 Connect your iPod to your computer.

2 Double-click the icon representing your iPod to reveal its folder structure.

Note: If you have set up your iPod to act as a storage device, you can find its icon in the Windows folder structure (it is assigned the next available drive letter); if you are using a Mac, its icon appears on the desktop and in Finder window sidebars.

3 Double-click the Notes folder in the iPod window.

4 Locate and select the text document that you want to be available for viewing on your iPod.

5 Drag the selected file to the iPod Notes folder.

The file is copied to your iPod.

6 To view the file on your iPod, select Extras in the main iPod screen.

Note: Remember to safely eject your iPod first. For more information, refer to the tip in the preceding task.

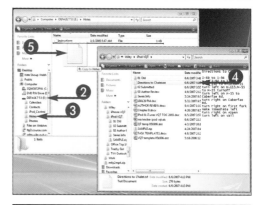

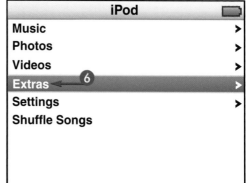

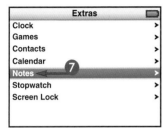

The Extras screen
appears.

⑦ Select Notes.

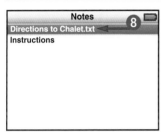

The Notes screen
appears.

⑧ Select the file that you
want to view.

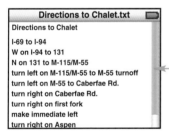

● The contents of the file
display.

Did You Know?
If you find yourself storing a lot of text files on your iPod, you can organize
them to make them easier to find by creating subfolders within the iPod
Notes folder. To do so, connect your iPod to your computer, and navigate
to the Notes folder as outlined in this task. Then create folders within the
Notes folder, applying meaningful names to each new folder.

Manage Your iTunes Library

Whether you have 100 files in your iTunes library or 10,000, you will likely want to find some way to manage all of this content.

One approach is to divide your files into multiple libraries. For example, you might establish a separate library for songs downloaded by another person to prevent those songs from playing in your library. This is useful if you have iTunes set to shuffle content or if you do not want those songs to appear on your iPod when you sync it with iTunes. If you like, you can set up iTunes to share your various libraries

with others — as well as allow others to share with you.

To ensure that you do not lose the contents of your iTunes library, you should regularly back it up onto a CD, DVD, or external hard drive. In the event that you switch computers, you can use this backup to port your iTunes library from your old computer to your new one.

Finally, if you share your library with others but you want to prevent them from accessing certain types of content, you can implement iTunes' parental controls.

Quick Tips

Suppose you share your computer with family members. How can you prevent your daughter's Fergie music from mingling with your Beethoven when you sync your iPod?

One way to do this is to create multiple libraries — one for each member of your family. Each library can be populated with files, whether they are on CD, stored on your computer, or purchased from iTunes or other online sources. Then, when you sync your iPod, you do this with your

own library to ensure that only your files are copied.

When you launch iTunes, it opens whatever library was in use the last time you ran the program. To open a different library, you can hold down the Shift key while you launch iTunes and, in the Choose iTunes Library dialog box that appears, click Choose Library. Finally, you can select the library you want to open and click Open.

① If iTunes is running, close it.

② Press and hold down the Shift key (Windows) or Option key (Mac).

③ While pressing the Shift or Option key, double-click the iTunes shortcut on the desktop.

Note: *If you do not have an iTunes shortcut on your desktop, launch it the way you normally do, such as from the Start menu or the Dock.*

④ Continue pressing the Shift or Option key until the Choose iTunes Library dialog box appears.

⑤ Click Create Library.

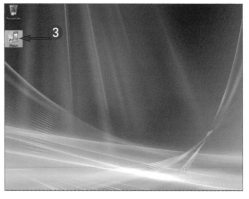

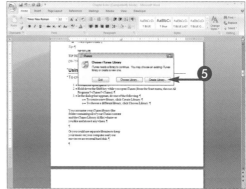

The New iTunes Library dialog box opens.

6 Type a name for the new library.

7 Click Save.

● iTunes creates a new, empty library.

Important!

A quick way to copy multiple files from one iTunes library to another is to locate the first library's iTunes Music folder (look in the Music folder on a Mac, or the Music or My Music folder on a PC). Select the files or folders that you want to add to the new library, and copy them. Then locate the new library's iTunes Music folder and paste the copied files and folders into it.

If your computer is connected to a network — for example, a wireless home network — you can share your iTunes library with as many as five other computers that are connected to the same network at a time.

When you share your iTunes library, others can enjoy the content that you have saved in iTunes — for example, listening to songs or watching videos that are in

your library. However, they cannot add your content to their own libraries, copy it to their own iPod, or burn it to a CD.

You can share content purchased from the iTunes Store, but only with computers that you have authorized to play your purchases. For more information about authorizing computers to play your iTunes Store purchases, see Chapter 2.

---

① Click Edit (iTunes on a Mac).

② Click Preferences.

An iTunes dialog box opens.

③ Click the Sharing tab.

④ Click the Share My Library on My Local Network check box (☐ changes to ☑).

● To share your entire library, select Share Entire Library.

● To share selected playlists only, click Share Selected Playlists.

● If you chose to share selected playlists only, select the check box next to each playlist that you want to share.

● If you want to require users to enter a password in order to access your shared content, select Require Password and type the password that you want to use.

⑤ Click OK.

iTunes reminds you that sharing is for personal use only.

⑥ Click OK.

TIP

Did You Know?

You can choose whatever name you like for your library; this is the name that displays to others when you share your iTunes content. To change your library's name, click Edit (iTunes on a Mac) and click Preferences. In the General tab of the dialog box that appears, type the desired name in the Shared Name field and click OK.

Just as you can share your iTunes library if your computer is connected to a network, others on the network can share their iTunes library with you. In order to do this, you must set up your own version of iTunes to detect shared libraries. When properly configured, iTunes automatically detects any shared libraries found on the network to which you are connected.

When others share their iTunes library with you, you can enjoy the content they have saved in iTunes — for example, you can listen to any songs or watch videos in their library. However, you cannot add their content to your own library, copy it to your own iPod, or burn it to a CD.

① Click Edit (iTunes on a Mac).

② Click Preferences.

An iTunes dialog box opens.

③ Click the Sharing tab.

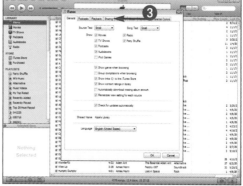

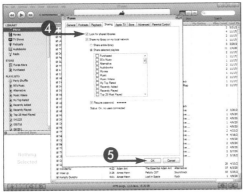

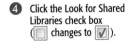

④ Click the Look for Shared Libraries check box (☐ changes to ☑).

⑤ Click OK.

● Shared libraries are listed in the Source list.

⑥ Click a shared library.

● You can view the shared library's contents in the File list.

Important!

If other users have purchased items from the iTunes Store, they can only share them with you if your computer has been authorized to play their purchases. For more information about authorizing computers to play your iTunes Store purchases, see Chapter 2.

Many people store hundreds or even thousands of files in their iTunes library, which represents a significant monetary investment. If those files are somehow lost or damaged, then replacing them can be not only costly, but time-consuming. To safeguard the files in your iTunes library, you should back them up on a regular basis; then, if disaster strikes, you can restore your iTunes library to its pre-catastrophe state.

You can store your library backup on CDs or DVDs. To do so, your computer must feature a compatible CD or DVD burner. To determine whether your computer is adequately equipped, you can open the Edit menu (iTunes menu on a Mac), choose Preferences, click the Advanced tab, and click Burning. You can then determine whether a drive is listed and, if so, how many and what kind. (Note that if you have multiple drives available, you are given the option of choosing which one you want to use.)

① Click File.

② Click Back Up to Disc.

The iTunes Backup dialog box opens.

③ Click Back Up Entire iTunes Library and Playlists (◉ changes to ◉).

● If, instead of backing up your entire library, you only want to back up purchases from the iTunes Store, you can select Back Up Only iTunes Store Purchases.

● If you have backed up your library before, you can perform an incremental backup (and save time and discs) by selecting the Only Back Up Items Added or Changed Since Last Backup check box.

④ Click Back Up.

⑤ Insert a blank disc in your computer's CD or DVD drive.

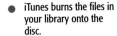

- iTunes burns the files in your library onto the disc.

Note: *If your iTunes library is too large to fit on a single disc, iTunes prompts you to insert additional discs as needed.*

iTunes notifies you when the backup is complete.

⑥ Click OK.

Apply It!

In the event disaster strikes, and you need to restore your iTunes library, simply start iTunes and insert your backup disc. When iTunes asks whether you want to restore from this disc, click Restore. If your backup consists of multiple discs, iTunes prompts you to insert each one in turn.

Transfer Your iTunes Library to Another Computer

If you purchase a new computer, you will almost certainly want to transfer your iTunes library onto it. Alternatively, you might like to have your iTunes content available on your work computer as well as your home computer. One way to do this is to use your iPod to copy the files over (if there is enough space on your iPod).

First you must enable your iPod to act as a storage device, as outlined in Chapter 8.

You should also consolidate the files in your library. To do this, open the Edit menu (the iTunes menu on a Mac) and choose Preferences, click the Advanced tab, click General, select the Copy Files to iTunes Music Folder When Adding to Library check box, and click OK. Then open the Advanced menu in iTunes and choose Consolidate Library.

COPY YOUR LIBRARY TO YOUR IPOD

1. Connect your iPod to your old computer.

2. If iTunes launches automatically, quit the program.

3. Locate the icon for your iPod on your computer.

4. Locate and select your iTunes Music folder.

   This is located in the Music or My Music folder on a PC or the Music folder on a Mac.

5. Drag the iTunes Music folder to the iPod icon.

● The iTunes Music folder is copied to your iPod.

Note: This operation can take a while.

6. Launch iTunes.

7. Click the ⏏ button next to the entry for your iPod in the Source list.

8. Disconnect your iPod from the computer.

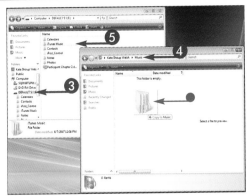

COPY YOUR LIBRARY TO YOUR NEW COMPUTER

① Connect your iPod to your new computer.

② If iTunes launches automatically, quit the program.

③ Locate and double-click the icon for the iPod on the computer.

④ Open the Music or My Music folder (Windows) or the Music folder (Mac).

⑤ Drag the iTunes Music folder in the iPod window to the My Music or Music window.

● The iTunes Music folder is copied from your iPod to the new computer.

Note: To free up space on your iPod, you should delete the iTunes Music folder after it has been copied to your new computer. To do this, click the folder in the iPod window and press Delete.

⑥ Launch iTunes.

● Your library is copied to the new computer.

Did You Know?

To transfer your iTunes library to a computer on which an iTunes library already exists, first consolidate the files on the new computer's library as outlined in the introduction for this task. You can then move the consolidated iTunes Music file to the new computer's desktop. After you transfer your library to the new computer, click File, select Add Folder to Library, locate the folder that you saved, and click OK to import those pre-existing files back into your library.

You can use parental controls to restrict access to certain types of content in the iTunes Store. Similarly, you can also implement parental controls within iTunes to prevent people with whom you share access to your library from accessing certain items.

The iTunes Store allows you to block content based on ratings assigned by such organizations as the Recording Industry Association of America, the Motion Picture Association of America, and TV ratings from the TV Parental Guidelines Monitoring Board. However, iTunes simply enables you to block access to certain types of items, namely podcasts, Internet radio, shared libraries, and even the iTunes Store.

① Click Edit (iTunes on a Mac).

② Click Preferences.

An iTunes dialog box appears.

③ Click the Parental Control tab (Parental on a Mac).

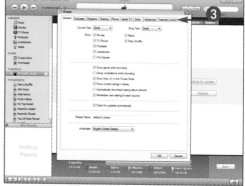

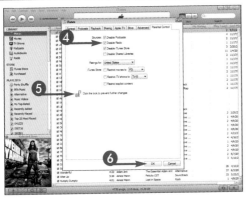

④ Click the check box next to each type of item that you want to block (☐ changes to ☑).

⑤ Click the Lock icon to lock your settings (🔓 changes to 🔒).

Note: When you lock your settings, anyone who attempts to change them is required to enter your administrator password.

⑥ Click OK.

● The items that you selected no longer appear in the Source list.

More Options

In addition to setting parental controls for iTunes, you also use this dialog box to establish parental controls for the iTunes Store. As mentioned, you can block content in the iTunes Store based on content ratings. For more information on setting parental controls for the iTunes Store, refer to Chapter 2.

Apple made iTunes extensible via plug-ins on both Macs and Windows. Mac users, however, can extend iTunes' reach via AppleScripts, Apple's system-wide scripting and enhancement technology.

You can use AppleScripts to create playlists, interact with other applications (such as Safari or Photoshop), as well as manage your tracks and albums. You can even use AppleScripts to search the iTunes Store based upon criteria from the currently playing track. Best of all, there are large collections of iTunes-related AppleScripts that can be downloaded and used at no cost.

① In your Web browser, navigate to http://dougscripts.com/itunes/. (The server is case-sensitive, so get the capitalization right.)

② Select a category on the left.

This example selects Controlling iTunes.

The category's selections appear.

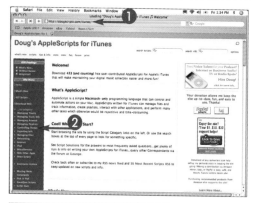

③ Locate a script of interest and click its download link.

Your Web browser downloads the script.

④ In the Finder, locate and double-click the downloaded file.

If the file was a zip archive, a folder appears and if it was a disk image file, a virtual disk mounts.

⑤ Copy the script file to the Library/iTunes/Scripts folder in your Home directory (create a Scripts folder if you don't already have one).

⑥ Start iTunes.

● iTunes opens and a new scripts menu appears in the menu bar with your newly installed script(s) in the menu.

More Options

Mac OS X Tiger and Leopard's Automator utility includes a number of iTunes actions, giving you even more ways to control your Mac's iTunes and iTunes content.

Index

Index

continued

201

Index

Index

Index

Index